Joe Sugg

GROW

Joe Sugg

GROW

Let's Go ~~Online~~ Outside

MICHAEL JOSEPH

PENGUIN
Est. 1935

Dedicated in loving memory of

Grandad Richard Chapman & Nanny Phyllis Sugg

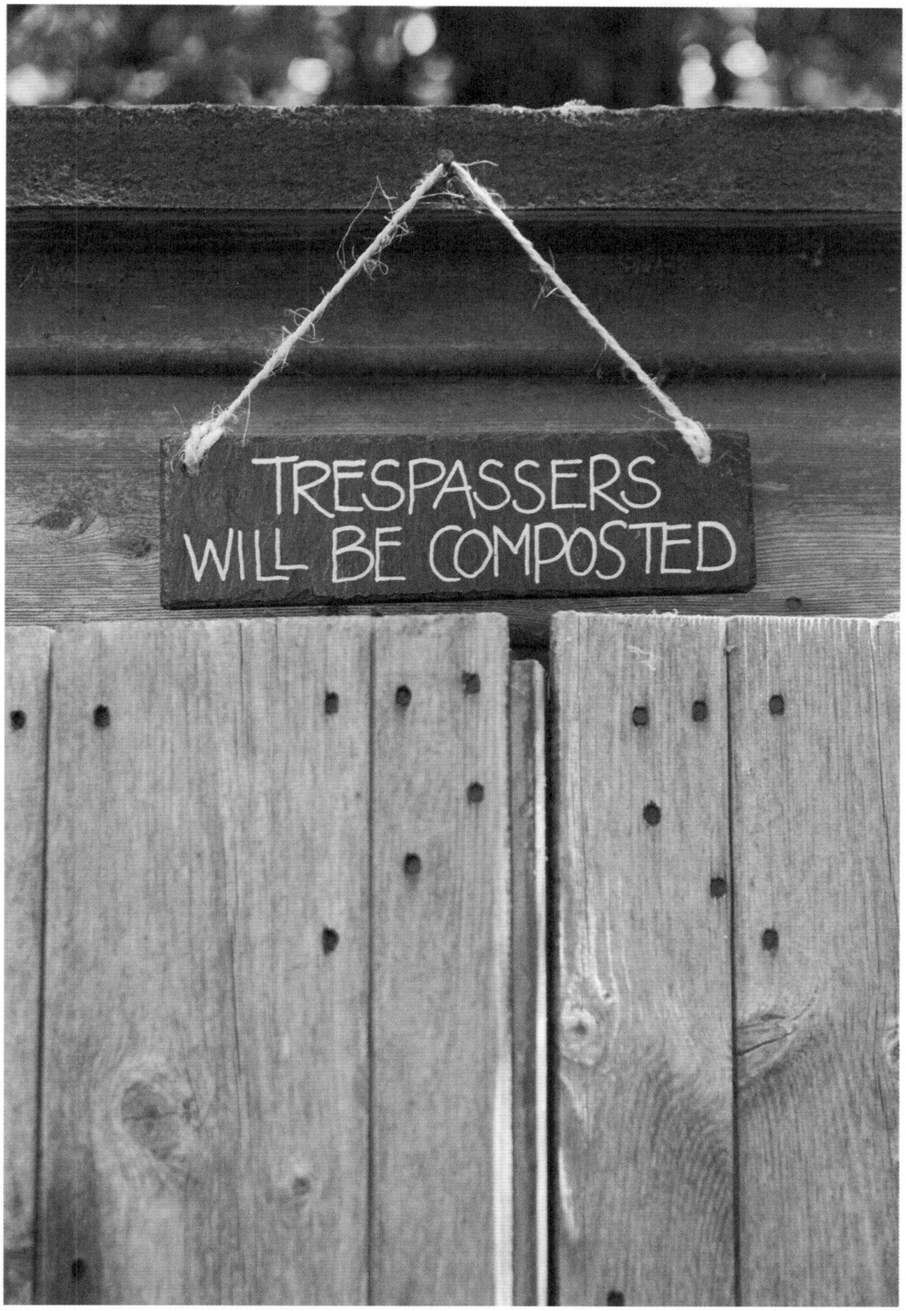
TRESPASSERS
WILL BE COMPOSTED

Contents

Intro

Little disclaimer before we start. The last time I wrote a body of work anywhere near to how long this book is going to be, it was an essay analysing Holden Caulfield's character in *The Catcher in the Rye* in year ten.

So, you might say I'm a little rusty!

But I knew that over the last few years I'd experienced something so life-changing and so life-affirming that I wanted to share it with you.

I've found that reconnecting with nature has helped me in more ways than I could ever have expected. Whether it's been long country walks, getting to grips with the garden, spotting wildlife or creating an oasis of calm via the medium of houseplants, I've fallen back in love with a world I'd lost touch with thanks to the fast-paced digital world I'd become so entrenched in.

It's had such a positive impact on my sense of self, my mental health and my overall happiness that I wanted to write it down, because it seems so simple now.

While I'd been searching for something which would do all those things, the answer was staring me in the face the whole time.

So, what is this book about? Well, at its heart, it's a practical guide offering you lots of tips and advice about how to invite more nature into your life and, hopefully, feel happier and healthier for it.

We're going to look at everything from gardens and outdoor spaces to wildlife and how to make the most of the world around us.

But it's also part-memoir because I think knowing a little more about my own story and how I ended up here might be helpful. With that in mind, I'm going to open up a bit about my childhood, growing up in quite an idyllic part of the world (although I didn't appreciate that at the time!) and always surrounded by nature.

I'm going to tell you how I fell into a digital career and how it consumed me in the best and worst ways possible. And I'm going to talk about how finding solace in nature has lifted me out of what was often despair and restored the balance and joy in my life.

As someone who has built up their entire career over the last decade using social media, I have seen it all. The trends that come and go, the new generations of content creators who arrive and change the game again – everything is in a constant state of 'blink and you'll miss it' progress.

I remember going to Facebook HQ in London soon after they had acquired Instagram in 2012 for $1 billion.

'Hey Joe,' I was introduced, 'meet Instagram!'

I turned around and it was just one guy sat at a small desk. That was Instagram. Oh, how times have changed since then.

But are we getting to a point where what assets you own in the metaverse matter more than what's going on in the regular old universe? Are we spending too much time sucked into the endless scrolling and creating a lifestyle that isn't healthy for us?

I myself have been exactly there and it's a rut. A pesky, deceptive rut.

Of course, social media, the internet and all things tech are not going to slow down just because poor ol' Joseph Sugg got addicted to his phone. And so it was down to me to do something about it.

I needed to find a balance between the fast-paced, internet lifestyle and the peace and calm of the real world where I could appreciate just being present in everything around me.

And rediscovering my love for the outdoors and the wonders of our beautiful, fascinating, messy, imperfect and extraordinary natural world, helped me make sense of a lot of what was going on in my head.

I'm hoping it may help some of you, too.

I'm not an expert in any of this; I'm still trying to understand this stuff myself by living it. To be honest, I reckon it might be a lifelong learning process rather than something you ever completely crack.

What I do have some expertise in, though, are the highs and lows of living your life online, and over the last few years I've worked hard to regain the balance which had slipped away from me.

So if you want to find out how I re-established my relationship with nature and managed to stop the scrolling and watching other people live their lives through beautifully edited montages set to catchy songs . . . you've bought the right book.

I'd love you to join me as we explore all of this, right from my early years which show why I've been deep-rooted in nature from a young age. Wait, did I just make a pun . . . already? Maybe I'm better at this than my *Catcher in the Rye* essay mark led me to believe!

Sorry. Tangent. You're going to get a lot of those.

Where was I? Oh yeah! I guess the overarching mission of this book is to help everyone, including myself, to find nature wherever we are and truly connect with it which, in turn, will encourage us to strike a balance between the online world and the real world.

So, make yourselves comfortable, put that phone on silent and let's see if we can GROW together. Wow, not only a pun, but also the name of the book in the closing sentence? Who do I think I am?!

Chapter 1

PRESSING PAUSE

I grew my first armpit hair at the age of twenty-one.

Not only is that the best opener to a book you've ever read (and for that, you're most welcome) but it's also true. Yes, that's right, I was the kid we all knew who defied the normal laws of biology and for whatever reason was a painfully late bloomer.

I'm not too bothered by it now as, of course, I did eventually get the eagerly anticipated growth spurt I used to dream of, and you know this because I've just announced the late arrival of armpit hair to the world via this book.

Anyway, I feel like I've used the words armpit hair three times more than I had initially intended so I'm going to move swiftly on.

It's not until more recent years that I've realized I've actually been a slow grower in other aspects of my life. I was the shortest and smallest boy in my year and I remember all the other boys being a lot quicker to shoot up in height. A few were even growing full-blown beards and looking older than some of the teachers . . . in year nine!

I always seemed to be playing catch-up to the latest trend or 'thing', as we called it. Although by the time I did, you can be sure that the bearded giants were already done with whatever it was and had moved on to whatever was next.

Honestly, I was OK with that. I didn't need the coolest new Lyle & Scott V-neck pullover, the latest Joop! aftershave or to know all the lyrics to the latest Kanye West song to feel like I fitted in.

I like to think that I made up for my lack of size with my social skills and being quick-witted enough to survive any playground teasing. I became a master in the art of self-deprecation and discovered that if I showed I could joke about the fact I was a little short-arse who couldn't fight his way out of a paper bag, people wouldn't think to poke fun at me in the first place. I was better at making jokes about myself than they were. Why put Joe Sugg in the bin if he can chuck himself in the bin and laugh about it?

Having said that, I did get thrown in a bin once, during a photography lesson, and yes, I did get stuck. Bizarrely, the culprit and I became best mates after this. I can't recall the reason for me ending up in said bin as it all happened very quickly and it was dark but (hi, Tom) I still haven't forgotten it. To be honest I think that was one of the tamer antics that happened in the school photography dark rooms.

Enter: the computer

Another thing I used to my advantage to compensate for being a slow grower was my ability to communicate online. At school I would get involved in conversations but I was much more of an observer. I liked to be a part of the discussion by listening to everyone else.

When I got home, however, things would change. I would race back as fast as I could and bolt straight upstairs to the spare room which, over the years, became 'the computer room'.

Our first family computer was a big, boxy, slightly yellowing white machine running the now-ancient Windows XP, and we got it when I was about ten.

"I'M HOPING IT MAY HELP SOME OF YOU, TOO. "

Now, for any younger readers, the computers back then were a lot more basic. It would take so long to boot up Windows that for a child with a short attention span (like me) it almost wasn't worth the fifteen-minute wait just to play *Minesweeper* and then cry because it didn't make sense.

FYI I still to this day do not know how to play *Minesweeper* and I don't think I ever will.

My sister Zoe and I used to have a rota for the hours we were allowed to use the PC – I would have 3:30 p.m. until dinner time and she would then be allowed to use it from dinner time until bed.

Over the next four years, computers changed a great deal. I still used ours a lot to play proper games (not *Minesweeper*), but by this time it was the early noughties and the internet had transformed the way we communicated with everyone.

We could now meet up with friends and interact with complete strangers in the Habbo Hotel or go into battle on *Age of Empires*. But even better than all this was the greatest piece of software available to any fourteen-year-old at the time.

I'm talking about MSN messenger.

If you don't know what MSN messenger is, then firstly I feel for you having missed out. And secondly, it scares me to think that there will probably be people reading this book who are too young to remember the days of rushing home to log into it to chat to the people you'd spent all day talking to at school.

This instant chat messenger even allowed you to see each other if you were fortunate enough to have a webcam. Although it was somewhere to hang out virtually with friends, it was also the place where all the teenage drama would go down – where it seemed people were happy to have it out and say the most awful things without having to look each other in the eye.

Even if you've never heard of MSN, you're probably reading this and thinking: 'hmmm, this sounds familiar'. And you would be completely right. This description isn't that far off what social media is like today for a lot of us. It was almost like younger me was anticipating what was to come through my big blocky computerized crystal ball.

I felt well connected on there. I could get my points across a lot better with more time to think of witty responses while behind the safety of a keyboard and in the comfort of my own home.

I would spend hour upon hour every day carrying on conversations and trying to see if my school crush would message me if I made sure I appeared offline and online again just so my name would pop up on her computer.

This era and the spike in social tech undoubtedly changed my life. But although I got sucked into this world of virtual hangouts and trying to get the girl of my dreams to notice me, I also had a switch in my head that would frequently go off telling me: 'Joe, you've been looking at this screen for too long; why don't you go outside and move a bit?' Initially I could silence this voice very easily and carry on nudging everyone on my contacts list. But I also noticed that spending too long staring at a screen, even though I was having a conversation (technically, at least), made me feel different.

I would get moody the same way you would if someone gave you a game to try and complete on the hardest level but then you just died over and over again and the frustration built up and you ended up chucking the controller across the room. That kind of feeling.

I was experiencing all this mixed with a sense of wastefulness which, with hindsight, I can see came from sitting in the same spot until it got dark. Realizing the whole evening had gone would then lead to regret and feeling like I'd missed out on more important things.

Conversely, I also noticed that if I headed into our local village after school rather than going home and getting online, it actually 'fixed' the feelings I was experiencing.

If I was going round to a friend's house to hang out in person, or having a kickabout on the village field or a game of hide and seek in the woods, that made me happier and more fulfilled than sitting on MSN or 'surfing the web' all evening.

Disclaimer: I didn't actually ever use the phrase 'surfing the web' myself because only people over forty said this back then to try and sound 'down with the kids' and I can assure you, down with us they were not.

But looking back on it now as an adult, it's very clear why inventing our own fun and entertainment held its own against new exciting tech. It was all about keeping a healthy balance between the two.

UK adults spend an average of six hours and twenty-five minutes in front of a screen – that's 40 per cent of our waking hours.

According to Ofcom, seven- to eight-year-olds spent an average of nearly three hours a day online in September 2020 and fifteen- to sixteen-year-olds nearly five hours.

Half of children own a mobile phone by the age of ten, and nearly all children do so by thirteen.

We now spend an average of a day a week online.

99.9 per cent of all children under the age of thirteen don't realize that an Etch A Sketch isn't touch screen. (I made that one up . . . but I bet I'm not wrong.)

Careering into the digi world

Fast forward to 2011 and my sister and her boyfriend Alfie gave me a gentle nudge into the world of creating my own content on YouTube.

I was an apprentice roof thatcher at the time and balancing that with this new interest in creating videos for strangers to watch all around the world was tricky. But it was manageable.

I couldn't quite believe that I was able to work five days a week up on the roof out in the fresh air, finally building some muscle on my small frame, and then spend the weekends growing a dedicated audience from my tiny bedroom. Life was great.

When I finally took the plunge and became a full-time content creator on social media, my life sky-rocketed and by the time I moved from rural Wiltshire to London with fellow YouTuber Caspar Lee in 2014 I was well on my way to two million subscribers and close to 100 million views. This quickly led to other opportunities involving big brand partnerships, television, meet and greets, creating our own film, red carpets, incredible events – and it seemed to go on and on.

It all happened so fast. One minute I was up a ladder essentially 'knitting' a roof and the next I was being invited to fly first class to Los Angeles to stay in a fancy hotel and go round Simon Cowell's house to interview him. I actually watched that video back recently and let me tell you, it oozes 'nervous country bumpkin WTF am I doing here, I don't know the first thing about interviewing anyone let alone Simon Cowell' vibes.

My life was the very definition of 'spinning plates'. It was autumn 2015 and I vividly remember my head being in the worst place it had ever been. Don't get me wrong, I am immensely proud and above all, extremely lucky to have had the career path I've had – I mean, what other job allows you to hang out with your mates and make content together for people who genuinely enjoy watching you?

It's a career where I get to be my own boss, too. When I worked for my uncle, he was self-employed, so I knew that every minute of work mattered. The quicker and harder you worked, the quicker you got paid and the quicker you were on to the next job. My career online was very much the same process. The more consistent you were and the more time and effort you put into it, the bigger and more successful it could be.

When it was night-time here in the UK, it was prime time for the Australians and Americans and many other countries across the world that I had accumulated an audience in. So the cogs were always turning alongside this constant want and need to keep up with everyone else.

For the first time, I never felt excited to start the day to create something fun to share with my audience.

Instead, I'd started to wake up with dread, fearing looking at my emails, knowing there would be a wave of reminders that certain content was due for this brand, oh and also this, that and all of those needed to be done before tomorrow for the film.

And all this against the backdrop of constantly scrolling through my phone, keeping an eye on what everyone else was up to in the world of the internet.

"THERE WAS A FEELING OF RELEASE, ALL THE NOISE AND URGENCY AROUND ME HAD DISAPPEARED. "

It was too much. I was completely swamped. I was still trying my best to please everyone and keep those plates spinning in perfect unison, but it just wasn't happening. I had completely burnt myself out.

I remember calling up Alex, my manager at the time, and saying: 'As much as I have loved this, I don't think I can carry on doing it any more.'

Alex did what she did best and managed the situation with a lot of reassurance. She even sent me a care package which contained bath bombs, blueberries, chocolate and a book. A book?! I hadn't seen a book in so long. But at that time it was exactly what I needed.

That night, for once I didn't immediately put my battery-drained phone on charge. Instead, I read the book from cover to cover. I'm a slow reader too, so that says something. It was *Harry Potter and the Cursed Child*, if I remember correctly – I probably thought reading about a cursed child might make me feel better about myself.

There was a feeling of release, all the noise and urgency around me had disappeared.

I knew it was only temporary and as soon as I charged my phone again it would all come crashing over me once more. But for the first time in a long while I had recharged my own battery, and that made an incredible difference in my mental state after being constantly online for work and pleasure.

It had become clear to me that the need for balance was essential. And it was going to take more than Harry Potter and a bath bomb to fix it.

Digital Detoxing

Taking a twenty-four- or forty-eight-hour digital detox can be a great way to (literally) unplug and give ourselves and our minds a chance to breathe. It's vital that we take time out to recharge our batteries and it's also a good starting point or gateway to exploring strategies to reduce or be more efficient with screen time in the longer term.

Tell friends and family what you're doing so (a) they don't send out a search party when you don't reply to the umpteenth WhatsApp message and (b) they can support you in your mission.

Choose a day which works best for you practically. For most people this will probably mean the weekend, but it should be a day you have the least need to be online and so are more likely to succeed.

Switch the phone off and shut it away. Same goes for the iPad, laptop and (if you're determined to go all in with the no screens thing) your telly.

Line up lots of activities to keep you occupied. Jigsaw puzzles, the Lego set you got for Christmas four years ago which has been gathering dust, journalling and books are all great. Take a long bath, cook a meal from scratch (er, probably best to print off the recipe before your detox begins!).

Think about the friends and family who you haven't had a proper catch-up with in forever and make a mental note to reach out to them when the detox is over.

Take some exercise in the fresh air and be mindful of all your surroundings as you do. So try to look up as you walk, noticing the clouds in the sky and trying to hear any birds that might be singing. It might sound silly, but noticing things in our natural surroundings helps us to really experience the moment, and for the benefits of being outside in nature to really sink in.

Keep a notepad with you to jot down any thoughts or ideas which might come to you now that your mind is clear.

Have a go at doing a little sketch in said notepad of your surroundings. Even if you're 'not a drawer'.

Go to bed at a sensible time and read a few chapters of your book before settling down to your zeds.

Make sure you have an alternative alarm clock set up if you normally use your phone! The more old skool the better in my opinion.

Getting off the scrollercoaster

I don't know whether this was to do with getting older, feeling a bit lost in the ever-growing, ever-changing world of social media, or just a sudden mental shift in priorities, but I had a lightbulb moment and admitted to myself that I thought I had an addiction to my phone.

Worse than that, an addiction to endless scrolling.

It might sound odd but when I hear the word 'addiction', my mind instantly goes to the image of somebody with a drink, drug or gambling habit who can't go a single day without their vice. I usually associate that image with someone looking worse for wear and in desperate need of help.

On that basis, I never saw what I was doing as an addiction and yet I was picking up my phone as soon as my eyes were open in the morning to scroll through social media, check the latest memes, read everyone's morning positive affirmation posts and see what people were having for their breakfast.

I would then look at the time and realize that I'd missed my own breakfast due to looking at everyone else's. Sometimes I would do the rounds of all the social media apps and then go back through them all again a few minutes later in case I'd missed anything, which is absurd.

My phone had become a comfort object for me and whenever there was a moment of waiting, like queueing in a supermarket, I found it difficult not to reach for it to fill that blank bit of time with some useless information. This made me feel a bit pathetic, like my willpower wasn't what I thought it was.

I started to overthink and feel a bit awkward and out of place if I wasn't scrolling to fill time.

After coming to terms with the fact that I was most likely a phone-scrolling addict I knew I had to make some changes. To begin with I decided to completely shut my phone off for a day. But sudden drastic changes and cutting things out are not the best thing for me to do and besides, I still needed my phone to work and be active on social media.

Instead, I needed to train my brain not to yearn to scroll. In short, I needed to be more present and give less of a shit about what everyone else was up to.

I started to use app limiters which are clever little features in our phones that allow you to set timers on certain apps. Just admitting this and writing it down is making me cringe at myself. I would allow myself thirty minutes on certain apps like Instagram and TikTok and by doing this, my usage would only be for creating and posting content.

However, there was one fatal flaw to this plan: the snooze button.

The alarm would sound signalling my thirty minutes were up and I'd think: 'Ah, just fifteen more minutes . . . oh go on then, another fifteen won't harm.' And before I knew it, I'd been hitting snooze for the rest of the day.

I'd failed. I couldn't even go a day abiding by the very rules I had set in place myself.

I've always considered myself to be someone with a very strong will. I hated getting told off at school and if I ever was, you can bet I wouldn't make the same mistake twice.

I've always applied this to life after school, too. If someone openly doesn't have belief in me or what I'm capable of, then I take it upon myself to prove them wrong. But more importantly, to prove to *myself* that my willpower is strong.

So when I had fallen at the first hurdle using the app limiters, I felt like I had lost one of the most powerful parts of my character. I set the limiters again, this time allowing a more realistic time (still thirty minutes for Instagram and TikTok but an hour for apps like YouTube) for a phone-scrolling addict trying to wean himself off his habit (baby steps, right?).

It was tricky, but when the alert popped up and my thumb inevitably reached for the snooze button, my inner voice told me off.

'Joe,' it warned, 'you've had your time, don't you dare press that button.'

I listened to that voice and stayed logged out. It was the first step in a long process, but I've since incorporated various other management techniques like using the 'watch later' tool for videos. This way, when I do have some well-deserved down time, I have a long list of videos that have caught my interest to choose from.

I started to become better and better at this. My screen time was decreasing and the screen time I *did* have was more productive, which left me feeling inspired and determined rather than deflated and anxious.

Setting some of these boundaries for myself between screen and the real world has improved my life beyond measure. I was learning how to prioritize my time on social media now and wasn't aimlessly scrolling but instead was being productive and updating my Instagram stories or posting a vlog on YouTube.

It improved my sleep, which I didn't believe at first as I'm quite good at falling asleep anyway, but it was more the quality of sleep was a lot better. I found that it helped with my conversation skills too and my attention span and patience improved.

Here are my top tips for reducing screen time

Don't sleep with your phone next to the bed – charge it overnight in a different room. Or:

↩ Way out of reach from your bed.

↩ Use an app limiter to tell you when it's time to step away.

↩ Use the Do Not Disturb feature on your phone. A lot of phones have different do not disturb settings for personal, sleep and work. Very handy. Very cool.

↩ Take up a hobby that doesn't involve a phone – by learning a new skill you're slowly getting used to shifting your attention to progressing in the hobby rather than on the screen.

↩ You'll want to tell yourself it's OK to search online to find 'inspo' for your new hobby and that's fine, but be strict with it. If you start scrolling aimlessly through stuff that has nothing to do with the task at hand, then stop and hang your head in shame, you naughty person, you.

↩ Make 'no screens at the dinner table' a blanket rule.

↩ At restaurants play 'phones in the middle' where everyone puts their phones in the middle of the table and if anyone touches their phone for any reason (unless it's an agreed reason by the table) they have to pick up the bill.

Think about areas of the house which should be unquestionably 'tech-free'. The bathroom might be one to start with.

Change your display to grey. Removing all the lovely colours from your phone makes looking at it less appealing. On the iPhone, go to Settings > Accessibility > Display&Text Size > Colour Filters and then toggle the switch to 'on' so you get the Greyscale option.

Android users can achieve the same by going to Settings > Digital Wellbeing > Wind Down and turning Greyscale on.

Set it up so you have to physically log in and log out of apps whenever you need to use them. This is such a pain in the arse it will definitely make you think twice about fulfilling that 'need' to scroll.

Turn those notifications off. I'm sure it's great that @superlikeyMclikerson1990 has liked your picture but do you need to know that in real time? Probs not. Disable those notifs, mate.

Try not to feel defeated if you don't manage to reduce your screen time the first time you try to. Keep going, try different techniques, and you'll get there – at the very least, you'll be in a lot healthier place just by noticing your screen time habits and trying to reduce it.

Too much information

There are probably parts of what I've spoken about so far which strike a chord with you. Most of us sit on the sofa in front of one screen with another screen in our hands.

Without getting all 'back in my day' on you, before our beloved family PC (minus *Minesweeper,* ergh), we would come home from school and play in the garden or watch kids' TV. There was nothing on until *The Simpsons* at 6 p.m. unless you were into *Neighbours* – I still find it odd that show was part of so many British children's growing-up process. Weird.

Anyway, the point I'm trying to make is that there was a fraction of the options of things to do and watch that we have today. And, of course, you have your trusty phone in your palm which also has access to infinite content to keep your brain busy.

Compared to even just ten years ago, we are worlds apart and it is now so easy to be distracted by – and addicted to – the technology we have at our fingertips. We're overloading our brains with so much information and not giving them time to take a break and digest what we're learning.

The effects of this have certainly impacted my life and I have seen first-hand the serious ramifications it's had on the lives of others around me, to the point where it makes me realize I was lucky to have come to terms with the fact I had an addiction and been able to act on it. I've had people close to me develop anxiety, stress and other mental health issues due to the pressures of social media.

Since I have improved my self-control, I've noticed how other people's relationships with their phones play out. I've lost count of the number of times I've met up with people for lunch or coffee and they've simply not been properly present because they're constantly checking their phones.

I've seen social media play a part in putting strains on relationships and also used to create drama between people. Pro tip from me: no one wins in these scenarios. I have yet to see a debate on the internet which doesn't end in someone not liking what they're hearing, failing to have a good comeback and so resorting to blocking the person with a different opinion to them.

That's a whole other chapter which I probably won't go into because we could be here all day! But we all know how those interactions can spiral and how exasperating they are. Seeing this darker side of social media emerge has shown me that so many of us find it difficult to establish and maintain boundaries while online and it's also this that has motivated me to make big changes to my day-to-day life.

By grounding myself back in nature, I can escape the noise and find tranquillity, and I hope by sharing my experiences, you too can find yourself in a healthier, happier and more balanced place when it comes to screens and being online.

Research by the Royal College of Paediatrics and Child Health shows there are very real health impacts of screen time on young people.

35 per cent of eleven- to twenty-four-year-olds said their screen time had a negative effect on their mood or mental health.

41 per cent said it had affected their play/fun.

18 per cent said it had a negative effect on family time and schoolwork.

Children with a higher screen time tended to have more depressive symptoms and more pronounced indicators of obesity.

Unexpected benefits of lockdown

I know after the last couple of years we've had, you probably don't want to hear me going on about the pandemic. But hey, you're nearly at the end of the first chapter so you may as well stick around for a bit longer!

The first lockdown was a really unusual time for me. I found myself stuck in my flat in London on about three or four group calls a day with various friendship groups. During the months we weren't allowed to leave the house, in between baking banana bread and watching *Tiger King* (wow, doesn't that feel like a lifetime ago now?), it seemed that despite not being able to leave the house, being online brought a whole new meaning to staying connected.

And in a weird way, it brought us closer together with loved ones.

Zoom remained a staple in keeping in touch for both business and pleasure, even as life returned to relative normality. I still to this day wonder what happened to poor ol' Skype, though. Growing up, Skype was the only thing to use really, to speak to loved ones via video when you were a long way from home.

As soon as a global pandemic comes along, the one time for Skype to stand tall and really have its moment, it was nowhere to be seen.

It's played on my mind ever since and I hope it's OK.

Anyway, back to the pandemic and the lockdowns. I don't know about you, but it made me appreciate my environment so much more. I was going on walks for my permitted daily exercise and stopping every couple of minutes to take in nature and appreciate how beautiful it was in its perfectly imperfect way.

Every walk became the highlight of the day. I was extremely envious of the people who had decided to invest in a houseboat pre-lockdown and were now sitting out on the top deck enjoying the empty River Thames with a barbecue going and a G&T in hand.

Even though we're lucky enough to be living in an age where technology is so good that we can see our families in real time on a screen, or sit on a beach anywhere in the world via a VR headset, there was something lovely about getting outside and embracing nature and restoring the balance I needed at the time. I'm sure you felt that too. For lots of us, getting outside, breathing in the fresh air and feeling that sense of freedom during the lockdowns was a vital part of our day – the part we really looked forward to. I reckon it was the first time many of us really understood quite how vital that connection to nature is for our wellbeing.

The digital generation

I can remember a time before smartphones and social media even existed – having to get creative to cure my 'boredom' has had its part to play in why I have ended up with the career that I've had.

But even though I'm not exactly ancient, it's hard for me to compare my childhood with what growing up in today's world is like. Studies have shown that children who have a lot of screen time, particularly over two hours per day, tend to have more depressive symptoms (although it has been found by some research that some screen time is better for mental health than none at all).

Another study also showed that 88 per cent of children and young people (aged eleven to twenty-four) said screen time had a negative impact on their sleep. This is the very reason I have been prescribed special blue light filter glasses to wear when looking at a laptop screen all day editing (or writing this book). These glasses are designed to filter out the blue light from the screen and can help reduce the damage caused by long exposure to it.

They also help me in my wind-down phase before bed as it's putting less strain on my eyes – blue light can also block melatonin, the chemical that helps your body prepare for shut-eye, so no wonder it has an effect on children's sleep.

We can't stop the advances in technology and it's only going to develop faster and more furiously. We now have generations growing up not having known life before the internet. And of course, it has enhanced our lives in so many ways. Look at the fundraisers, the community building, the job creation and the space which has opened up for everyone to use.

It would be silly to say that the internet, our phones and social media aren't helpful. But it's so important to check in with ourselves and others around us to find and maintain a healthy balance of screen time and real-life experiences and interactions.

This is the digital age and, like it or not, social media plays such a big part in everything we do now, but little changes can be made here and there to maximize your happiness and wellbeing while continuing to use these incredible tools.

Learning and understanding how to be present and take joy from your surroundings is vital – knowing when we need to disconnect from the tech in order to reconnect with the people and the world around us. And the great thing is, we have a remarkably powerful antidote to the stress and pressure of our screen-obsessed lives literally on our doorsteps. The more you can get outside in nature, or bring the natural world into your home, the more balanced you will feel.

I'm not saying I have this whole thing figured out, not by a long way! But over the course of this book I will share some of the tips, experiences, learning curves and boundary-setting that have helped me over the years, and perhaps together we can make a bit more sense of it all.

Chapter 2

NATURE & NEURONS

When it comes to defining myself, I will always proudly declare that I'm a country boy. I mean, at the age of eleven I got scolded by a mob of angry parents for throwing sheep poo at all the other children at a party, and if that doesn't scream country through and through, then, quite frankly, I don't know what does.

In my defence, it was old, dried sheep poo, so I really don't know what all the fuss was about. If anything, given how on trend everything organic is nowadays and depending on who you ask, it's probably good for you! I was ahead of my time – they should have thanked me!

I was very fortunate to grow up in a small village called Lacock in the beautifully rural county of Wiltshire. I say fortunate, but if you'd asked me as a teenager if I enjoyed living in a small chocolate box village, you'd have received a very different, much more stroppy answer. But we'll get to that later.

We moved house a few times as children but never more than a stone's throw from the previous place. I remember when I was aged six moving to a tiny hamlet next to Lacock called Reybridge. This house was surrounded by fields which had a river running through them and if you live next to a river, you're going to get the wildlife that comes along with it . . . including rats.

So I grew up pretty unshielded from nature and I've carried a love for it all the way into adulthood. Today I appreciate it in ways I could never have understood as a child and I'm going to be sharing some of its positive impacts on me as we go through this chapter.

Regardless of what's going on in my life, connecting back to nature never fails to bring me comfort and relief, and I know I'm not alone because the latest science backs me up. Regardless of where we grew up, all of us instinctively understand that being in nature is powerfully good for us.

There's actually a term for the idea that, as humans, we have an innate instinct to connect with nature and other living forms: biophilia. The word first came about in the 70s and was coined by US-based psychoanalyst Erich Fromm who described it as 'the passionate love of life and of all that is alive'.

American biologist Edward O. Wilson took the idea of biophilia further a decade later and proposed that humans' affinity with nature and other life-forms was partly genetic.

There is certainly something both grounding and reassuring in being reminded that no matter what, something bigger is happening out there – the world keeps spinning, the flowers keep blooming and the seasons keep changing.

According to mental health support charity
Mind, bringing nature into our everyday life can:

improve mood

reduce feelings of stress or anger

help us feel more relaxed

improve our physical health, confidence
and self-esteem

connect us to our local community
and reduce loneliness

Anyhow, this old house, the one that appeared to be home to the whole cast of *The Animals of Farthing Wood*, also had an INCREDIBLE back garden. At the time it seemed to go on and on forever, and what blew my little mind even more was that there was an actual maze at the end of it. That's right, we had our own maze!

Before you all get too excited at the idea of young Joe living it up in his own private maze like a Wiltshire version of Richie Rich, it was actually just a load of long grass the previous owners hadn't bothered to mow. My parents decided to trample it down and create this 'maze' for us, but when you're five years old, a maze is a maze, right?

I would spend hours and hours (mainly because I wasn't good at mazes and would get hopelessly lost) on my hands and knees crawling my way around trying to find the centre, creating characters in my head who would join me on this quest to track down my missing toys in an ultimate rescue mission.

My memories of that homemade maze in the garden will never leave me – in fact, I remind myself quite often that some of the best fun I had as a child came from using my imagination and creating entertainment out of my surroundings. Remember, this was pre even Sega Mega Drive times.

The best we had as kids were Pogs (little round discs that had a cool picture on and were usually given out for free in bags of Walkers crisps); a gooey alien that came in an egg full of slime but basically did nothing (although there was a rumour – never confirmed – that if you managed to squeeze two aliens in one egg it would create a baby); and, if you were really lucky, a robotic, irritating nightmare otherwise known as a Furby.

My parents were creative and taught me the games they used to play as kids using the environment around them. Games like Pooh Sticks, where you all stand on a bridge and drop a stick on one side and run across the other side to see whose stick comes out first. Or Forty Forty In, which is a game where you all have to hide somewhere and try and get to the designated base location and shout 'Forty forty in!' followed by your name without the defender spotting you first and beating you back to the base and shouting 'Forty forty out!'

OK, this game is super complicated to explain on paper, but if you ever meet me out and about, I'll be happy to elaborate and maybe even play it with you if the conditions are right.

What all these games had in common was getting us out, exploring the countryside and interacting with nature. And we were doing this without even realizing.

According to government statistics:

90 per cent of adults surveyed in May 2020 said natural spaces were good for their mental health and wellbeing.

Over 40 per cent noticed that nature, wildlife and local green spaces had been even more important to their wellbeing since the coronavirus restrictions began.

Creepy crawlies

The Sugg Family Walk was often the last thing I wanted to do, especially as I approached my, ahem, 'difficult' teenage years, but it would always end with a spring in my step as opposed to the stompy march I would start it with. There was something about being outside in the fresh air, being observant about what was going on around you and its beauty and stillness that I absolutely loved. Still do.

Sometimes we'd go for walks and not say much at all, instead just listening to the sound of birds and the wind in the trees. Other times we would have really engaging conversations about life, school, future plans and funny stories. I would come home feeling a lot more motivated and filled with ideas about what I wanted to do with the rest of my day.

My sister and I also used to walk the mile to school with our mum most days in the warmer months. One crisp spring morning, aged five, I discovered a recently deceased maybug on the pavement.

Fun fact for you here. Because I'm writing a proper book, I felt the need to double check that it was indeed called a maybug and it turns out it's actually called a cockchafer. I wish I'd known this when I was in school as that would have been hilarious for my immature mind.

Anyway, these beautiful creatures are very large for an insect and do look quite intimidating. My mum explained their life cycle to me and that they only live for between five and seven weeks, and it baffled me, even at that age, that something so impressive probably wouldn't have lived as long as the summer holidays.

I pleaded with my mum to let me collect it off the pavement and take it to school so I could share it with the other kids and teach them what I'd learnt about this doodlebug. She agreed and I marched my way into the school proudly showing it to everyone and, sure enough, I had a crowd of mesmerized classmates peering at what I had in my hands.

To be honest, most of them ran away in terror, but a handful stayed and learnt a bit about nature from me. I loved that and it kickstarted a real fascination with all the minibeasts that roamed our garden.

Even now I can't go for a walk and pass a log without giving in to the urge to turn it over to see what lives underneath it or to see how close I can get to observing a bee collecting pollen without losing my squeaky clean record of thirty years alive and zero stings! Argh, I hope this hasn't jinxed me.

The coolest minibeasts to spot in your garden or park

Water Scorpion

Not a real scorpion although this underwater predator looks very similar with its front pincer legs used to catch prey. They hang about still-water ponds and lakes and you can spot them all year round.

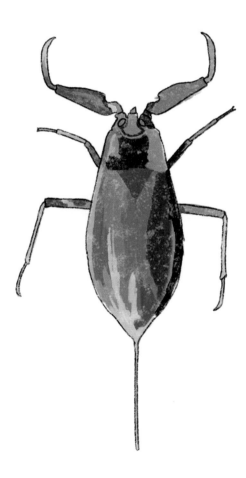

Rose Chafer Beetle

Warning: these blighters will destroy your rose beds! But they really are stunning to look at with their metallic green wings.

Violet Ground Beetle

A black beetle with a purple twist! These guys have a striking violet edge all the way round their wing cases and thorax. When I say wing cases, they don't actually fly, but they can run super fast. They're nocturnal so you'll have to be up after dark with a torch to find them, but they are very common in flower borders, compost heaps and herb gardens.

Garden Tiger Moth

With their furry red and black bodies and bright red hind wings, garden tigers are very distinctive – spot them in gardens around July and August. Or if you're like me, keep an ear out for them when they fly into your room in the dead of night and you think it's a ginormous hornet come to end you . . . it was quite traumatic.

Mayfly

Mayflies have been around for more than 300 million years – they were here even before the dinosaurs! They tend to be grey-bodied with long, thin abdomens and almost lace-like wings. Spot them all year round – they like hanging out wherever there is freshwater.

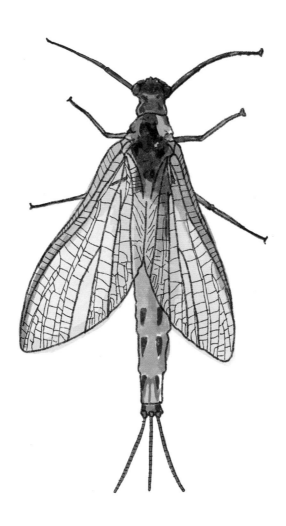

London calling

Growing up surrounded by fields, sleepy villages and maybugs was a million miles away from the capital city where everything felt so fast-paced and anxiety inducing. I had only visited London once on a school art trip to the Tate Modern in year ten. I discovered two things on this day.

1. I loved art and felt very inspired by what I'd seen.

2. I didn't like London. Not one bit.

I'm a people-pleaser and just felt like I was in everyone's way as they were rushing to get to various places. I remember getting home to the safety of my village and thinking that it didn't matter where life took me, you wouldn't catch me going *there* again in a hurry.

So, when I actually *did* move to London in my early twenties it was because life had taken me in a very strange and unpredicted direction.

I lived there for seven years in the end and, this may surprise a lot of you given what I've just said about the Big Smoke, I loved every single minute of it. It was such a learning experience throughout my twenties.

There was always some sort of event going on or some cool new place to go and check out and I made so many friendships there. But eventually, with the big Three-Oh approaching and the global pandemic (sorry for bringing it up again), I started to re-evaluate what I wanted in life not just for me but for my partner too. By this time, Dianne and I had been together for a couple of years after meeting and being partnered together on the 2018 series of *Strictly Come Dancing*.

I think what really prompted the change was seeing that I could continue with my work and what I loved doing from home. Which, in turn, started me thinking about exactly *where* felt like home for me.

Whenever I went back to Wiltshire, the air felt fresher, you could see the stars at night and going to sleep without hearing a siren blaring or a train going past every five minutes felt like a gift.

I also noticed that I felt so much more relaxed in this slower-paced place and that I'd get the same feeling I remembered from the end of the family walks. I had time and space to think about my future and all the exciting things and projects I'd like to work on, and I'd feel refreshed and ready to throw myself into a big project.

Or I'd have the confidence and energy to take on something I'd normally be too scared of and end up regretting that I didn't do.

It dawned on me that all this wasn't just because I was back in my hometown; it was being back in the countryside itself that made me feel recharged and re-focused and above all else, less stressed.

Dianne felt the same. She grew up in what is essentially the Australian version of the countryside, only they have wild kangaroos hopping about the place rather than a single dead cockchafer on the pavement.

A few of the best wildflowers and where to spot 'em

Name: Houseleek

Features: Fleshy leaves and red spiky petals

Where they live: By roadsides or on walls

When they flower: June–July

Name: Cornflower

Features: Intensely blue flowers blooming from a scaly cup

Where they live: Cornfields and bare ground

When they flower: July–August

Bonus Fact: This flower can be pretty good for your skin. It regulates sebum production. Could be one to whack in your nightly skin care routine.

Name: Ragged Robin

Features: Pink, raggedy petals on top of a forked stem and narrow, pointy leaves

Where they live: Marshes and anywhere damp

When they flower: May–June

Name: Purple loosestrife

Features: Upright hairy stems and leaves with violet-coloured flowers

Where they live: Streams, rivers and marshes

When they flower: June–September

Bonus Fact: You can actually use this plant in tea to help with diarrhoea. Although, be warned, searching for this plant in the garden when nature calls can be stressful.

Name: Bluebell

Features: Clusters of bell-shaped blue/purple flowers with tips that curl back

Where they live: Woodland

When they flower: April–May

Name: Bloody cranesbill

Features: Gorgeous pinky-purpley petals and hairy stems

Where they live: On cliffs and sand dunes

When they flower: June–August

Name: Honeysuckle

Features: Sweet-smelling climber with creamy yellow flowers, often with a tinge of orange or red

Where they live: Hedgerows and woodland

When they flower: May–August

Bonus Fact: These things smell incredible. You often smell them before you see them.

Name: Foxglove

Features: Trumpet-shaped flowers drooping down one side of an upright stem

Where they live: Open woods and hedgerows

When they flower: June–September

Bonus Fact: I used to be scared to go near these plants as there were always bees hiding in the flowers waiting to sting me (or so I thought).

Name: Cow Parsley

Features: Tall, hollow-stemmed plant with sprays of pretty white flowers

Where they live: Along basically every roadside . . .

When they flower: May–June

Bonus Fact: I was always told as a kid if you or a horse ate this plant you would die. I never had a desire to do so, and I never owned a horse, so I have no way of knowing if (a) this is true (I'm assuming not) or (b) why I was even told this . . . weird.

A country boy again

It was just before the third lockdown in January that we packed up our busy London lives and went from a house in the city to a home in the countryside.

Of course I questioned our decision, though. Several times.

'Joe, you need to be in London if you want to succeed in the industry you're in!' I'd tell myself.

'Why?' I'd reply (to myself). 'London social events give you anxiety and you get ridiculous imposter syndrome walking down red carpets worrying about what people are thinking of you!'

I'm not the best networker in the world (I wish I was), mainly because I'm surprisingly shy around new people and find small talk very awkward.

Another nagging question was: 'But Joe, won't you get bored?'

But the answer to that is, as I've since discovered: far from it. How could you get bored when there is endless countryside to explore and beautiful views to take in while still having connections to reach nearby towns and cities?

Also, having the extra space here means friends and family come and stay. Dianne and I like to think of ourselves as decent hosts and the idea of creating a space that's ideal for having guests round to take a break from their busy lives and come and chill out has become really important to us.

I have good internet out here and as it's easier to stay connected to people, technology is making it feel less important for me to be in London. When I do need to go there for work, I enjoy a commute on the train as it's time to myself to put on a good playlist and zone out (if I can get a seat).

We even have Deliveroo in rural Sussex! Yes, out here in the middle of nowhere we can still order food straight to our door.

The change has taken me a little bit of time to get used to, but being able to get back in the open air and appreciating nature has been one of the best decisions I've made.

And I fully believe that mentally, the move came at exactly the right time.

The following organizations are a great starting point if you're looking for more information on where to find nature near to you or ways of getting involved in nature-based projects.

wildlifetrusts.org

A grassroots movement of people with a mission to restore a third of the UK's land and seas for nature by 2030. Wow!

gov.uk

The government's own website has lots of info about nature reserves, green spaces and where to find them.

nationaltrust.org.uk

Find walks, parks and estates local to you.

rhs.org.uk

The Royal Horticultural Society is the UK's leading gardening charity.

farmgarden.org.uk

Discover local farms and community projects.

wwf.org.uk

The World Wildlife Fund has some great advice on their website about how to find nature on your doorstep.

canalrivertrust.org.uk

Dedicated to looking after the country's waterways – lots of projects going on across the country.

nationalparks.uk

The most beautiful landscapes the UK has to offer and where to find them.

ngs.org.uk

The National Garden Scheme lists gardens open to the public across England and Wales.

woodlandtrust.org.uk

Protecting trees, woods and wildlife, they are the caretakers for over 1,000 woods across Britain.

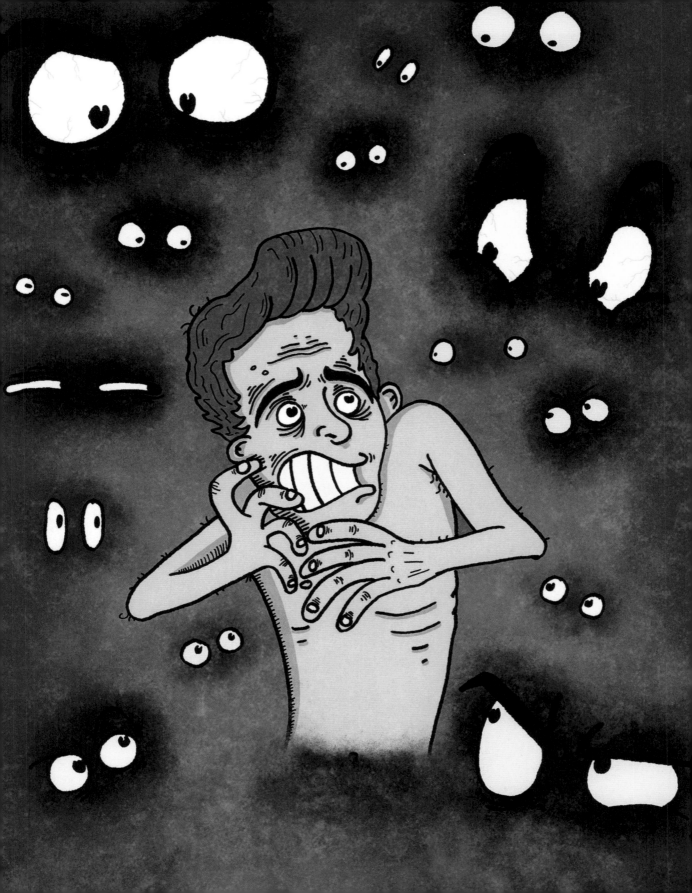

The mind games

As most of you will know, mental health awareness has grown massively in recent years. Growing up, I never really knew anything about it and it's incredible to see how much we have progressed when it comes to understanding it and doing more to help those in need.

Like most people, I've had my highs and my lows in life. I'd never felt anxiety or panic before, but I knew a lot about it through Zoe who suffers from it. So, I'd learnt what to do if someone I knew was having a spell of anxiety or a full-blown panic attack, but I didn't know what to do if it happened to me.

Lo and behold, it eventually got me. It was about two years into being an 'online personality' and I started to get this overwhelming sensation which seemed impossible to escape. It came in different forms, sometimes irregular breathing, or the feeling that I was going to vomit, and always claustrophobia.

It was like being completely trapped, and what made it worse was that it would usually come on whenever I felt stuck in conversation with someone or at a group dinner – places where it would feel rude if I just got up and left to get away.

I'd certainly never experienced these feelings when I was up on a roof in the rain . . . so why now? Turns out, when you have the attention and expectation of quite a lot of people who watch your videos, it can sometimes feel too much.

When you think about it, human beings probably aren't meant to meet so many new people in their lives. We're probably evolved to know the people in our tribes or villages and a few others, and that's it.

So it was a strange time learning to cope with that in a big city – bear in mind that I have imposter syndrome too, which is when your mind doesn't let you believe you deserve or have earned your success.

Thankfully, it wouldn't happen to me that often, but when it did, I would have moments, like I mentioned in the last chapter, when I wondered if only I'd stuck at the thatching, I might be in a better place mentally.

To make it worse, along with these occasional showers of anxiety and the tidal wave of imposter syndrome, there was an approaching tornado of something else entirely.

Oh hello, comparison and self-consciousness.

I'm lucky in the sense that I have never been self-conscious of my physical form, but mentally and in work I went through a self-destructive stage of secretly comparing what I was doing to other people in the same field.

This would lead to me scouring social media to check in on what everyone else was doing to see how my own work measured up. I started to pride myself on being 'the one who comes up with unique video ideas' which, for a while, worked really well!

I found an old game called Telephone which I saw on an old TV comedy improv show called *Whose Line Is It Anyway?* A phrase would get passed down a line of people who would be wearing headphones playing loud music, meaning they would have to rely on lip reading to pass the message on.

It usually ended up being a very different sentence to the original, often with hilarious results.

I wondered if I could bring this back and turn it into something new for an online audience. I thought people would enjoy it. And they did!

It went viral and other creators from all over the world were also making videos doing the same thing – it even ended up being played on *The Tonight Show* with Jimmy Fallon in the States multiple times with some of the biggest A-listers in America like Will Ferrell, Keanu Reeves and Margot Robbie.

Typical! I was barely two years into my exciting new career and I had 'peaked'. I'd come up with something that had become bigger than just me, which in a weird way had always been the goal.

Now I needed to keep this up and make every video I put out better than the last which, obviously, is quite unrealistic.

TURNS OUT, WHEN YOU HAVE THE ATTENTION AND EXPECTATION OF QUITE A LOT OF PEOPLE, IT CAN SOMETIMES FEEL TOO MUCH.

This led to huge pressure, constantly comparing myself to others, and left me feeling exposed and self-conscious creatively. I didn't care if people had something to say about my appearance or anything like that, but if someone said that my latest video wasn't up to standard . . . well, that cut deep.

I'm telling you all this, but I don't want you to reach for your miniature violins and feel sorry for me at all! But an over-consumption of social media definitely had a direct impact on my mood, motivation and happiness.

So, I need to take steps to counteract all this. I've never really been much of a morning person, but getting up early and going for a walk or a run before the rest of the world wakes is so good for me. I find a sense of calm in myself and also time to think about ideas for future projects, things I want to accomplish and the people I've not spoken to for a while, reminding myself to check in with them to see how they're getting on.

No matter how busy and crazy our lives and minds may feel sometimes, everything feels easier and more peaceful when out in nature.

A good playlist can be the difference between going for a run and . . . not going at all! Music helps motivate and inspire me to run farther and faster. Here are my failsafe running anthems:

'Ocean Drive'
Duke Dumont

'Firestone'
Kygo

'Sad Machine'
Porter Robinson

'Walking with Elephants'
Ten Walls

'Afterglow'
Wilkinson

'Panic Room'
Au/Ra and CamelPhat

If I'm going for a Personal Best or I just need that extra 'oomph' to change gear, these are the tracks which work for me:

1. Guerrilla Radio -
2. Breed - Nirvana
3. All my life - Foo F
4. Club Foot - Kasabi
5. You're gonna go far
6. Bleed it out - Linki
7. Seven nation army
8. Edge of Seventeen
9. Welcome to the Jungl

Finding nature in the city

You don't have to live in the countryside to feel the benefits of nature. There is so much of it in urban settings – it's just that you might have to look a little harder at first.

When we lived in London, I would go for walks and runs along the river or in our local park in Battersea. Sometimes I'd just go out and wander. Everyone else would be in their sports gear meeting a personal trainer, walking their dogs, or doing any number of obscure activities you'd only ever find in London.

But I was there for none of those things. I would find solace just looking around and thinking of what I wanted to do with work, relationships, family.

Finding and making time to do this for ourselves once a day really helps clear our heads. Even if you don't have access to a local park or green space, just getting out there – anywhere! – for a stroll can have a really positive impact. Wherever we are in the world, it's really important to build into our day windows where we can get outside into nature. These moments will restore, rejuvenate and bring us perspective when we need it most.

How to discover and appreciate nature in the city

Start a nature journal, take it with you everywhere and be ready to jot down observations, feelings and thoughts at any point when you're out and about. And whatever the weather!

This journal is for YOU so it can be anything you want it to be. Record the flowers you've come across, the animals or birds you've spotted, tree or leaf rubbings or how sitting in a peaceful spot makes you feel. Also, if you're not much of a writer, sketch what you see!

Keep track of the birds who visit your garden or local park. Each year the RSPB runs its Big Garden Birdwatch which is the world's largest wildlife survey and is free for everyone to join. Go to rspb.org.uk for more info.

There are some great apps which help us identify flowers, plants and wildlife. Seek by iNaturalist is a bit like having a miniature David Attenborough in your pocket and uses image recognition to tell you exactly what you've stumbled across.

Head to water! Whether it's a lake, pond, stream, marshes or river, there is guaranteed to be all sorts of wildlife to be found.

Find a nearby community garden and see if they're looking for volunteers to help with its upkeep (spoiler: they definitely will be!). Go to rhs.org.uk to find out more about your local area.

Take a trip to your nearest wetlands – work is ongoing to restore, re-establish and create them, especially in urban settings over recent years, because the environmental benefits are undeniable. Wetlands are areas covered by water, providing unique ecosystems and a refuge for all sorts of plants and wildlife.

There are many brilliant organizations such as the Wildfowl and Wetlands Trust working to preserve our wetlands and build new ones – visit wwt.org.uk to find out more about what they do.

Exercise outdoors. It's much cheaper than the gym! Do we always need to take the bus or local train? Every now and again, walk instead and really take in all your surroundings as you do.

I recall once having a very stressful, full-on day of work at the same time I was preparing to be in the West End musical *Waitress* in 2019. I'd just finished my final rehearsal and had a moment of sheer panic. The security blanket of time was up – this was it. The next time I'd be performing what I'd been rehearsing it would be the real thing in front of a giant crowd of passionate theatre-goers expecting a good show for their money.

It made me feel a bit sick with nerves. But rather than jump on the busy Tube or take a car home, I decided to pop in my earbuds and put on some relaxing classical music. I walked from New Oxford Street all the way down through Covent Garden to Embankment Pier. People were whizzing by in a dash to get home during rush hour, but me? I felt unusually calm.

Even though it was a drizzly dark evening in September, I took my time, and during that walk, I managed not only to calm down my busy mind but also remind myself that despite the nerves, I was going to get through it, put on a good show and people would enjoy it.

Some people are gifted with thinking positively like that all the time and go their whole lives always seeing the best possible scenario rather than the worst. Reader, I am not one of those people. I'm the sort of person who gets on the plane and immediately looks for the emergency exit before eyeing up all the other passengers and working out a plan of action in case of disaster.

This trait has, unfortunately, sometimes held me back from letting go and enjoying things in the moment and I reckon I've missed out on some good experiences because of it.

I've never experienced a 'proper' rollercoaster (the teacups are usually my limit) because in my mind I've already analysed all outcomes that could go wrong. What if the ride gets stuck? What if my seat falls out? What if I pass out? Wouldn't be the first time, that's for sure. What if someone throws up and it lands on me and then because of that what if I'm sick and it lands on someone else? What if I'm just simply queuing up to go on a ride and one of those annoying vloggers drops his GoPro mid loop-the-loop and it lands on my head and I suffer memory loss and mislay all my fondest memories from the last thirty years?

See what I mean?

So for me, having this moment plodding along the wet cobbles of Covent Garden where my brain was helping me in a stressful situation rather than jumping on the bandwagon of bringing me down, felt like a huge turning point.

Hey, I would be lying if I told you that moving to the countryside and buying myself a pair of wellies and a wax coat has fixed everything. I still have my wobbles here and there like a normal human.

But gaining this sense of calm, the renewed sense of perspective nature brings, and having a bit more space in which to grow, has put me in a much better place. And it has undoubtedly helped me be more present and focused on the things I want to achieve in life.

Chapter 3

THE GREAT OUTDOORS

'Are sharks more likely to eat you at dawn in Brighton?' is one of the many weird and wonderful things I've found myself Googling recently. And I'm going to tell you why.

The piercing sound of my alarm went off at precisely 4:45 a.m. and, while I might be wrong, I'm convinced that the earlier you set your phone to wake you, the louder the thing seems to go off.

So, thanks for that parting gift, Steve Jobs.

The reason my alarm was waking me at such a disgusting hour of the morning was because I had set myself a task – one that *should* be very simple but in reality is pretty difficult. My task was to *carpe diem*. In other words: seize the day.

I opened my puffball eyes and instantly rolled over to fumble for my phone and attack the snooze button with my sleepy limbs, but the alarm continued. I remembered that my phone no longer lived rent free on my bedside table – it had been banished to the other side of the room.

Someone once told me that it's not good to sleep too close to your phone at night, especially if it's on charge. And I only know one person in the whole wide world who doesn't charge their phone at night (yes, I'm talking about you, Dianne!), which always ends in stress when her train tickets are stored on there and she's down to 1 per cent battery.

But, as we already know, I had fallen into a nasty habit of endlessly scrolling before bed, actually to the point where a public service announcement would pop up warning me about over-consumption of screen time. I would feel the guilt creeping its way from my phone, through my hands all the way to my brain.

It would make me put my phone on the table and then, funnily enough, I'd go on to have a very restless sleep which would then lead to my hitting snooze too many times the following morning and consequently feeling like I'd not made the most of my day.

As you can see, this is a classic example of a slippery social media slope. So I made the bold move to put my phone on the other side of the room, out of reach and temptation's way.

Anyway, back to my bitey, sharky, Brighton story. I left the comfort of the warm Joe-shaped imprint in the bed and stumbled all bleary-eyed to stop my phone assaulting my ears, got dressed in the dark (which is actually fine because the chances are, at such an early hour, there won't be any other humans around to notice what you're wearing), plodded downstairs and headed off to the beach.

I'm not the most confident driver. I am a good, sensible driver, just not very confident. It's something to do with the people-pleaser in me and always being worried that someone's going to beep at me which will play on my mind while I figure out what I've done wrong before realizing that I wasn't ever in the wrong and it was actually just an impatient idiot in a rush.

Being up this early though, the roads are pretty much empty – in fact, the entire country is pretty much empty. Don't get me wrong, I like people, but if you don't like people, then trust me you need to make the most of this very special part of the morning!

The reason for my early morning trip to the beach? Paddle boarding.

Climbing a-board

I received a paddle board for my thirtieth birthday from my sister Zoe and her boyfriend Alfie and I instantly knew that it was going to be a real treat of an activity and one which ticked all the boxes.

Stand-up paddle boarding is one of the fastest-growing water sports in the UK and its popularity exploded during the height of the pandemic, which doesn't surprise me as it's a superb way to social distance from literally everyone!

It's also great exercise. Just keeping your balance on one of these things gets all your micro muscles working and properly sorts out your core. Then you're paddling through the river or sea so you're also working your upper body.

I don't want to put anyone off paddle boarding by making it sound like a military workout on water, because it's really not like that at all, and this leads me to the main reason I love it. It's SO relaxing and peaceful.

The sea is usually as calm as it possibly can be early in the morning and late in the evening, and there are also fewer people around, which means not too many witnesses when you inevitably lose your composure (and a bit of dignity) and fall in!

There's something about gliding across the still water silently, taking in your surroundings and giving yourself as much space as possible, which is so special to me. It really is the perfect way for me to start my day.

I have a special waterproof bag which I store my phone in, but it's very rare I'll get it out. Partly because, knowing my luck, it will send me off balance and I'll take the plunge, but mainly because I find it such a wonderful time to breathe in a bit of nature and enjoy the scenery.

When I was researching this book, I read that watching the sunrise is very good for mental health and releasing endorphins, and I can tell you, watching the sun come up while I'm filling my lungs with fresh sea air really gives me time to clear my mind, think of new ideas or even try a bit of meditation.

Meditation for me is a love/hate relationship as I have such a busy mind and it's taken me years to get anywhere near good at it. Even now I'll still have rogue thoughts rudely interrupt with things like: 'Are sharks more likely to eat you at dawn in Brighton?' which usually then gives way to frantic Googling and then, before I know it, I'm completely distracted and sucked in by a documentary on how they made *Jaws* look so real way back in 1975.

For the record, there aren't any sharks in Brighton, just in case you were wondering. And so, safe in the knowledge I'm not going to get torn limb from limb by an angry great white, I can slip into the perfect zone of giving my mind a much-needed rest. The whole experience has me coming back to the beach with a real sense of reinvigoration and accomplishment.

Although it's painful to hear that alarm go off at such an ungodly hour, if you can push past the temptation to hit snooze and just get out there before the rest of the world wakes up, your body may hate you, but your mind will thank you for it.

You may even feel slightly smug that you've managed to achieve something before most people have even thought about what they're having for breakfast.

I'd really encourage you to give the sunrise paddle boarding a go (finish this book first as, despite my diva-like demands to the publishers, it's probably not waterproof). You can search your local area for companies that run sessions on rivers, ponds, lakes and the sea if you're lucky enough to live near the coast. You can hire everything and it's a pretty reasonable cost too. Thank me later.

There are loads of outdoor activities besides paddle boarding with proven mental health benefits which will have us all basking in nature. You might want to give any of the following a whirl . . .

Wild swimming

A survey by social enterprise Swim for Good found 82 per cent of swimmers reported mental health benefits from open water swimming.
Go to outdoorswimmingsociety.com for more info on how to get involved.

Trail running

Get off the pavements and take your runs to the mountains, the fells and open green spaces. There's a wealth of guidance out there but runnersworld.com is a good place to start.

Rambling

Research by YouGov found nearly 90 per cent of respondents agreed that walking in nature helped them unwind and relax. For details on walks local to you, visit ramblers.org.uk.

Kayaking

Exercising on water can have a direct link to a reduction in anger, depression and stress. Gopaddling.info will help you find activities and clubs in your area.

Geocaching

This is basically the coolest ever treasure hunt and it takes place right across the country. You are given clues provided by people who have hidden 'caches', and seekers use GPS to find them. It's the best example I have seen of combining technology and getting outdoors and enjoying nature. It can take you on all sorts of weird and wonderful trails. Go to geocaching.com for more info.

How to make the most of your time outdoors

Take photos of where you've been and who you're with and start making a scrapbook of your new adventures. Make sure you're wearing the right kit. There's nothing more miserable than plodging along with cold, wet feet.

Plan ahead and research some of the areas near to you that you'd like to get to know a little better. Local Facebook groups are a wealth of information, advice and tips for this sort of thing. So is Instagram. Search the place or tags of the places you're intending to go, and you will see where other people have taken the photos that show off that location the best.

Don't feel any pressure to 'do' anything once you're out there. Sometimes just 'being' in nature is all you need to truly relax and unwind.

Happy campers

I've always been a fan of camping holidays. If you know me and have followed my life for a while, you'll be aware of the fact that I'm the very proud owner of a beautiful 1966 split screen VW campervan called Chippy, named after my grandad.

I've driven Chippy on quite a few trips to the New Forest and even to Glastonbury with friends and family. It's loads of fun to drive, especially as there is so much space to fill with passengers and other essentials and a seat in the back where someone can give me a shoulder massage while I'm driving (honestly, I think that could be the best thing about it).

One of the reasons I've always been so keen to own one of these amazing vehicles is because of all the childhood holidays spent camping down in Dorset, Devon and Cornwall.

My uncle, aunty and cousins had a campervan and would regularly go on trips down to the coast to live that #vanlife for a week or so and I'd often get invited to join them.

Camping holidays were a different kettle of fish to sunshine breaks in the Algarve. There was no all-inclusive, no swimming pool and certainly no guaranteed blue skies or warm breezes. Instead we would arrive at the site, park up the van and then spend a good few hours trying to understand the instructions for putting together the tent, before deciding that whoever wrote said instructions and designed this stupid tent was doing a Steve Jobs-esque loud alarm wind-up trick.

When the tent was finally looking vaguely stable (upright, at least), we'd then get the small gas cooker going or fire up one of those disposable barbecues and all chip in and cook food together.

I'm not a chef by any means, unless I've just followed the instructions from one of those food box delivery services like Gousto or Hello Fresh – then I think I'm Gordon effing Ramsay. But the food was always that easy comfort grub such as chilli con carne or spag bol, and by the time it was ready on the painfully slow little hob, you'd be struggling to see what it was you were eating unless you were smart and had packed a head torch . . . which I obviously hadn't.

But it's these camping trips which are, without doubt, some of the most memorable and enjoyable holidays I've been on, and I didn't even need to leave the country! Being outside, exploring some of the UK's beautiful locations and spending quality time with friends and family in the process is priceless to me.

And I came to realize that even when you're trying to erect a tent in the sideways rain, or when a seagull swoops down and steals the food you've just been cooking for four years on the tiniest stove in Cornwall and it feels like Mother Nature is having a good ol' laugh and picking on you, it's these memories that stay with you forever.

If you're not used to roughing it, here is a foolproof list of camping trip essentials to get you started . . .

SLEEP

All-weather sleeping bag

Pillow

Mat

CLOTHING

Waterproofs, waterproofs and more waterproofs

Base layers because it can get COLD

Decent, emergency thick skiing socks because, as I mentioned above, it can get COLD

Hat and gloves

Plenty of clean underwear

Sensible, robust footwear

KITCHEN

Stove or BBQ

Fuel

Cool box

Kettle (essential!)

Bottle opener (even more essential!)

Tin opener

Pots and pans

Plates and mugs

Cutlery

Tea towel

Washing-up liquid

Water carrier

KIT

Mallet

Spare pegs

Batteries

Penknife

Torch

Matches

Rubbish bags

First aid kit

Duct tape

Hand sanitizer

Insect repellent

Camping chairs and table

TOILETRIES

Toothbrush and toothpaste

Soap and shampoo

Towel

Wet wipes

Toilet roll

Suncream (you can dream)

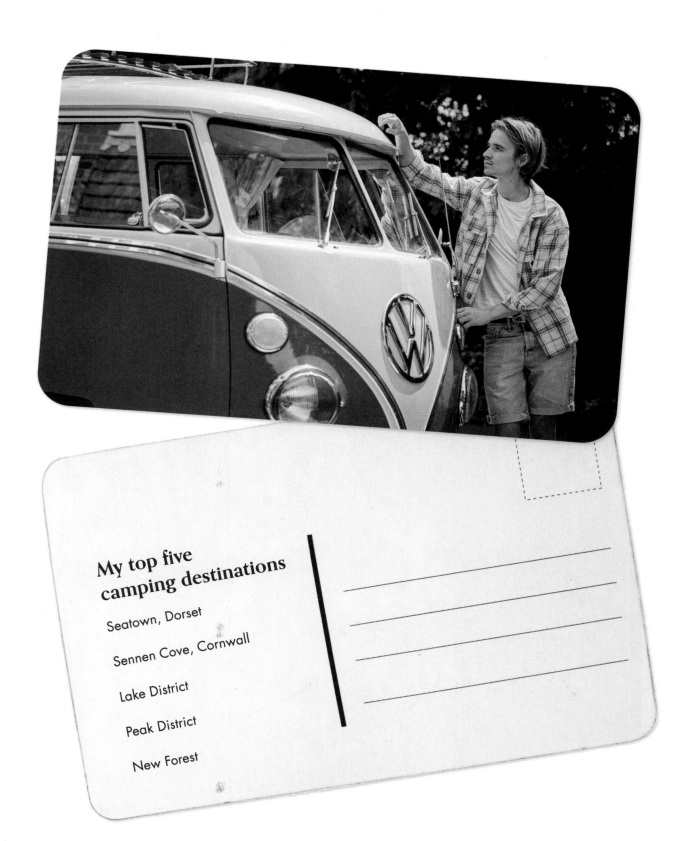

My top five camping destinations

Seatown, Dorset

Sennen Cove, Cornwall

Lake District

Peak District

New Forest

Clearing the cobwebs

Getting out and about has also helped me when going through difficult times. We've all been there. You've had a falling out with your parents over something ridiculous and you stand up tall and with a big bellowing voice announce: 'I'M RUNNING AWAY FROM HOME', followed by stomping up the stairs to try and make one of those polka-dot-handkerchief-on-a-stick things a la Gromit in *The Wrong Trousers* when that evil penguin started making his life hell. Poor Gromit.

Anyway, you would very swiftly realize that you don't in fact own a polka dot handkerchief or have a stick handy and so you make do by grabbing your *Star Wars* backpack and stuffing in your 'essentials' (which, at seven years old, is just your *Street Sharks* and *Biker Mice* toys, your Tamagotchi and all your remaining sweets) into it.

I tell you, if Bear Grylls had been about back in the 90s he would've been shaking his head, probably while simultaneously taking a big bite out of a badger or something.

The actual 'running away from home' would be a moody plod down to the bottom of the garden or to the end of the driveway to sulk until you inevitably calmed down and made the short journey back, realizing that there's not an awful lot to do when you run away from home . . . there's no Sega or Nintendo out in the wild.

As funny as it is now to look back on those kinds of memories, I still do this as a thirty-year-old man, just dressed up in a different way.

To this day, if I'm ever feeling a bit down, been given a bit of bad news, had a disagreement with someone or even just when I get that 'eeerrgh' feeling when you've been inside all day looking at a screen (sorry, that's the only way I can describe it, but you know what I mean, hopefully), I'll stop and acknowledge to myself what's going on here and do the same thing I would as a child.

I run away from home.

These days it's not to make a point to my parents or cause them to worry that I've gone missing so I get a bit of attention. Instead, it's to clear my mind, make everything seem less busy and to make myself generally feel a lot better mentally and physically.

I started off doing this back when I lived in London by going for walks along the Thames River Path. I would pop in my AirPods and put on some calming music or a funny podcast and take in the people and everything going on around me.

Taking time to go outside would have a positive knock-on effect with everything else I had going on that day. Because of my busy schedule, I used to think that taking time like this would be counterproductive and I'd be using the walk as procrastination to put off starting something I should be cracking on with.

But in fact it allowed me to think with much more clarity and not feel so overwhelmed with having to spread my time between so many different new projects in an industry that was forever changing.

After moving to the countryside I carried on with these walks, still listening to music or podcasts but also taking time to pause and switch off the headphones and just sitting and listening to the sound of nature. I think it's often easy to forget how lovely it is to stop and be quiet for a while and take in the soft breeze, the birdsong and the rustling leaves.

I must admit, I nearly had a little cringe writing that sentence, but it's true! I've lost count of the number of times when I feel like I'm starting to get stressed or down about work and a walk outside has reversed my mood.

I've started taking a notebook and a pen with me and finding a bench in the middle of nowhere surrounded by sheep with incredibly large testicles. I never knew a sheep's ball bag could be that big! Can you give me a better definition of taking in your surroundings and learning from nature? I'll wait.

I'll sit there in the field of these well-endowed sheep and jot down my thoughts, goals, worries and how I'm feeling about life generally. This journalling has worked wonders for getting mental clarity and aligning my focus with what's important, and it's also great for looking back on and telling myself that I *am* making progress in life. Even if it's little steps.

Sometimes a chilled-out playlist is the perfect accompaniment to a stroll in nature. My top tracks . . .

WHY DO BIRDS FLY THOMAS J. CURRAN

ALONE IN KYOTO AIR

CIRCUS BONOBO

HOLOCENE BON IVER

RAIN THOMAS J. CURRAN

HEARTBEATS JOSE GONZALES

HERE COMES THE SUN THE BEATLES

BREAKDOWN JACK JOHNSON

PINK+WHITE FRANK OCEAN

CONCERNING HOBBITS HOWARD SHORE*

*(I like putting this on and pretending I'm a hobbit off on an unexpected journey . . . so what?)

JOE'S CHILL-OUT PLAYLIST

Here comes the rain again

Now, this all sounds like I know what I'm talking about, and I've got this great little set-up going and I'm sure you're picturing me frolicking through a field with sheep with . . . ahem . . . and those cartoony Snow White birds chirping around my head.

But it's not always like that.

If you live in the UK, you know that the weather needs no explanation. It's our go-to talking point and it also ruins almost any outdoor event, seemingly on purpose. I'm blaming Steve Jobs for that one, too.

But hey, if you can't beat it, join it. And for me, I've decided to embrace it and now, quite literally, come rain or shine I will still head out for a walk when I feel I need one.

I've grown to really enjoy a walk in the rain. Yes, really! If you're properly prepared and decked out in appropriate clobber, there's often no better time to get out there because you basically get the whole place to yourself.

I spent some time at the start of 2021 in multiple bidding wars on eBay trying to become the proud owner of a classic wax coat so I would really look the part. I eventually won a bid-off and not only do I love my new get-up, it also gives the house a faint smell of wax coat as you walk in which always reminds me of my nan and grandad's.

Dianne, on the other hand, has taken on a less traditional countryside look and gone for what I can only describe as Boho-country-chic. Bright orange Wellington boots . . . with a heel! And all covered in the sort of patterns you'd see on the wall in a yoga studio.

The good thing is, with those bright boots and bright red hair, it's almost impossible to lose her in a woodland or cornfield.

The wax jacket is perfect for a walk on a drizzly day and I find the sound of pounding rain and the smell of the wet earth really calming. Personally, it further increases mental clarity and those feelings of inner peace and contentment.

Getting the wellies on is, for me, akin to putting two rubber army tanks on your feet. It allows you to explore everywhere people with ordinary shoes simply can't go.

Hopefully I've convinced you that being active outside whatever the weather doesn't have to be torture. And if you're still on the fence, then I'm about to push you off, because there's science that backs up what I'm saying! Being outside, whether it's just for a quick walk or a full-on training sesh, is proven to be beneficial for our mental health and wellbeing. Research shows it helps lower blood pressure and those pesky stress hormones and even helps us get vital vitamin D which most people in the UK are deficient in, especially during the winter months.

Getting outside for any reason releases endorphins which keep all kinds of mental health issues like anxiety and depression at bay.

To me it's not rocket science – it all makes perfect sense! I guess you could say that the 4.45 a.m. paddle boarding alarm was a wake-up call in more ways than one.

Chapter 4

GARDENS & OUTDOOR SPACE

OK, I know what you're thinking. 'Wait, Joe Sugg has a whole chapter in his new book about . . . gardening? When did he go from being a young internet guy to a nature-loving, green-fingered fanatic, snapping at the heels of Alan Titchmarsh and Monty Don?'

Listen, I get it. If you'd asked me what a hydrangea, chrysanthemum and clematis were a few years ago, I would have told you that, quite obviously, they were the three main characters from a Tesco Value version of *Harry Potter*. Or three diseases you could potentially catch from not reheating rice properly the day after (yet again) overindulging and ordering too much Chinese takeaway the night before.

But you'll be pleased to know that now, at the grand old age of thirty, not only do I know what these three things are (they're plants, by the way) but I've also learnt the wonder and frustration and a plethora of other emotions that come with looking after your own personal outdoor space.

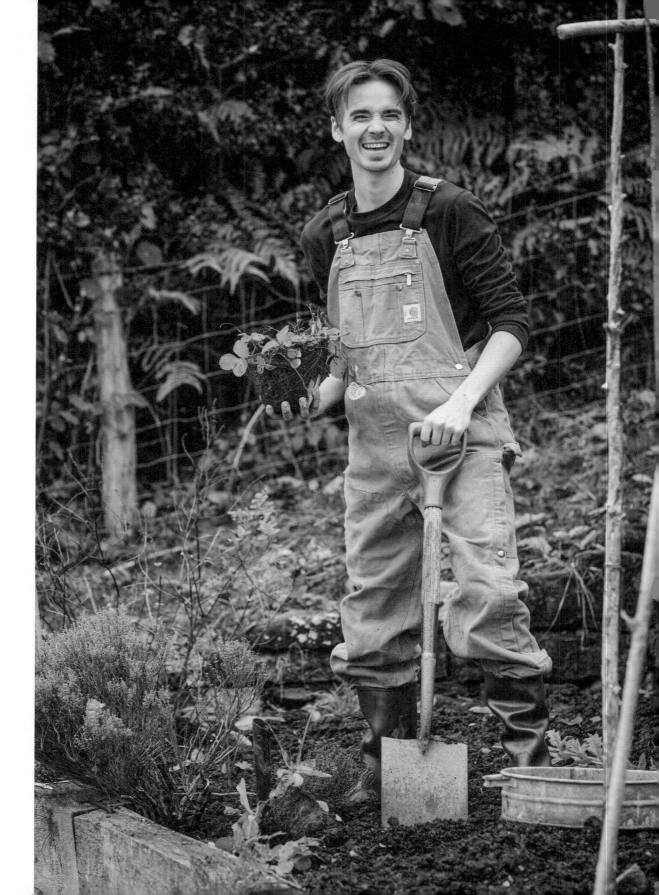

Falling in love with gardening

When I was younger, I never truly appreciated how much effort and time went into making our family garden the wonderful place it was. As a teenager, I used to find plants boring. Plants weren't going to get you a girlfriend, or to Level 55 on *Call of Duty 4*, and they weren't going to top up your phone when you'd run out of credit.

I never thought for one minute I'd ever get to the stage where I would become invested in creating my own perfect outdoor space for my future family, but life can take some funny turns, and just like that weird magical moment when you reach adulthood and all of a sudden you like olives, I have become quite the amateur gardener with a passion for all things horticultural.

I'm lucky enough to be writing this overlooking a big sloping green canvas which will be that future garden. I say future because we don't quite know what to do with it yet. I find that living in the twenty-first century when you have Pinterest and Instagram at your fingertips to dribble over 'garden porn', gives you a sense that anything is possible.

I'd be lying if I said the garden wasn't a big factor in what made us want to move here. I felt excited about creating our own version of what I was fortunate to have growing up, and one day having our own children enjoying it.

You really don't need a shed full of fancy tools to be creative in the garden. If you're just getting started, here's what I'd recommend you kit yourself out with – and remember it's worth having a look on local buying and selling sites and Freecycle, especially before investing in spanking new items.

1. A good pair of gloves. Thick enough to protect your hands and wrists from prickles but not so bulky that it makes it tricky to handle the more delicate plants.

2. Secateurs or hand pruners

3. A sturdy spade

4. A hand trowel, preferably made of stainless steel for durability. This will be your new best friend when it comes to potting, weeding and planting.

5. A garden hose will make keeping everything watered so much easier. Invest in a watering can too so you can top up anything that needs a drink in between your hosing sessions. Or if you have the space, a water butt.

6. A garden fork – these can dig into soil better than a spade and make the ground good and ready for planting.

7. A hoe will help clear weeds much faster than doing it individually by hand.

8. A rake to clear away cuttings and leaves

9. A kneeling stool. Your back will thank you.

My first family garden

I remember so vividly the day I went along with my mum for the first time to visit an old red-bricked, derelict house which would become our family home for most of my childhood and teenage years.

'Mum, I don't like this. Why are we moving here!?' I whinged, staring at the big, mouldy, gaping hole in the ceiling above the even mouldier kitchen sink. It looked like the kind of place where you almost certainly would catch a nasty dose of clematis.

Mum reassured me and explained that Dad was going to work on it and turn it into a beautiful home with no rotting holes in the ceilings and that I would even have my own bedroom, which was a major deal-clincher for me as I'd spent my entire life up until this point sharing a room with Zoe.

I took an instant shine to the garden. It was a good size, completely overgrown and even had a small stream running alongside it. My imagination kicked in and I transformed into a young Indiana Jones, cutting his way through the jungle vines with his machete looking for an entrance to a hidden tomb full of treasure.

In reality, it was swishing a stick in the long grass in rural Wiltshire, and unlike my hero Indie, I never did find that entrance to a secret treasure tomb. But what I did discover was something way cooler to a six-year-old – a decapitated fox head!

I'd never seen anything like this before in my life, and here it was in our new garden! While the new place was being renovated, we temporarily moved into the other house I mentioned earlier (the one with the grass maze) and when we finally returned to the now-mould-free red-brick home, I couldn't wait to see what else I could find in the garden.

The possibilities seemed endless!

I have picked up a number of lessons about gardening over the years. These are the most important (er, maybe):

* Don't mess with those little orange centipedes you find in the soil or under rocks. They may be bright orange but that doesn't mean you get a free pass to touch them or interfere with them in any way as they can get evil and ruin your day. They bite and it HURTS.

* Same goes for earwigs. Initially, I wanted this whole chapter to just be me slagging off earwigs, but that probably wouldn't have been fair of me. Because despite how much I loathe these little critters (I once innocently touched the abdomen of one when I was younger and discovered that those big pincers do some kind of scorpion movement to pinch your finger and make you cry), they're actually so good for the garden. They're great for the compost heap and they also eat the pesky aphids and mites who are intent on destroying those nice new plants you just spent a fortune on at the garden centre.

* Don't learn to ride a bike in the garden if your dad's just dug a massive hole for a pond close by. I feel like I don't even need to explain this one. You get the picture.

* Get down and dirty with your soil type. Knowing whether it's clay, sandy, chalky or loam will help you decide what is most likely to thrive in the garden, and the easiest way to check is by hand.

Clay:

sticky when wet and can be rolled easily.

Best for: perennials and shrubs, especially roses, hydrangeas and geraniums.

Sandy:

gritty, will run through your fingers and can't be manipulated into shape.

Best for: bulbs such as tulips and hibiscus as well as veg like carrots and potatoes.

Chalky:

dry and crumbly with lots of stones – hard to dig!

Best for: lavender, viburnums and lilac as well as spinach and cabbage.

Loam:

fine and slightly damp, this is a mix of sand, silt and clay (the optimum ratios are 40 per cent sand, 40 per cent silt and 20 per cent clay) and is the best all-rounder.

Best for: pretty much anything – loam provides the most desirable conditions for plants and flowers to grow in.

A photo album with wallets makes a great filing system for your seed packets so you can have all the info you need right at your fingertips.

The best time to water the garden is first thing in the morning as this is when the sun is coming up, allowing your plants and flowers to get the most out of the lovely drink you're giving them.

Raised beds or containers are good solutions if you're short on space. Facebook Marketplace is a brilliant resource for getting hold of these very cheaply.

If you go through a 'cricket phase' after England win the Ashes one year and it inspires you to become the next Freddy Flintoff, it will ruin the grass and annoy your parents.

If you go through a 'rugby phase' after England win the World Cup in 2003 and it inspires you to become the next Jonny Wilkinson, it will ruin the grass and annoy your parents.

However, the main thing I learnt about having a garden was that thanks to the hard work, care and patience of my parents, it became the most beautiful space and would go on to host barbecues on hot summer days and the best ever Easter egg hunts.

It was the place we hung out in the tiny Wendy house which was always full of spiders and where we'd draw Pokemon with school friends on the musty off-cuts of carpet from the house renovation. Sometimes we'd just chill out in the hammock under the pear tree.

It was also the place we would pitch a tent and camp out with friends, doing prank calls and playing spin the bottle (I was better at the prank calls).

The garden for me, was – and still is – a place that I hold very close to my heart. And I always found calm and distraction there which took my mind off any not-so-great times I was going through.

Five easy as pie barbecue favourites

1. **Burgers** (obviously) – the big, slightly more expensive ones that don't shrink to the size of a pound coin as soon as they hit the grill.

2. **Hot dogs** – I'm pretty sure it's borderline illegal to not include sausages on a barbecue, right?

3. **Corn on the cob** – controversial one, but when else in my life do I get to eat a huge bit of corn with my hands? Never, is the answer, unless it's at a barbecue. Slightly charred with butter and salt . . . perfection.

4. **Potato salad** – one for my veggie and vegan friends but also a staple barbecue side dish, especially if they're your grandad's home-grown new potatoes.

5. **Banana split** – you know, where you put chocolate in a banana and wrap it in tin foil and barbecue it. It shouldn't work but it does!

The Great Olive Tree Drama

Before moving to the countryside, Dianne and I lived in an apartment in London where we had small outdoor spaces which were very manageable. Like a lot of people, I got the gardening itch about one month into the first lockdown.

If we couldn't go outside-outside, then I would bring the outside to us!

I recently read an article that showed some of the most bizarre lockdown purchases and it was brilliant – people were buying anything from inflatable bars to karaoke machines.

I didn't think I was the sort of person to get sucked into this manic world of purchasing wacky stuff, but my 7,541-piece Lego Millennium Falcon says otherwise.

I did, however, make what I think in retrospect was a very smart lockdown purchase.

Olive trees.

I already had a few olive trees which had survived four winters and even produced actual olives in the summer, so I knew that these new additions to the family would fit right in.

Where they didn't fit was the apartment lifts. Somehow, I had to get these six-foot olive trees up to the top floor of the block and, to make it worse, due to the pandemic, the use of elevators in our building was actively discouraged. As a self-confessed rule nerd, I didn't want to get into trouble.

Besides, as this was during a time where it seemed like every day there was a new set of unclear regulations, I wouldn't have been at all surprised if somewhere in there was one stating: 'No more than one person in an elevator at a time and this includes oversized olive trees that are clearly too big for your apartment, Joe Sugg, you silly boy.'

Nevertheless, I wasn't going to be defeated. It took me the best part of a swelteringly hot day but I heaved those olive trees one at a time all the way to the top of that building, squeezing them through the front door and past Dianne who was in an important Zoom meeting.

It can't have looked very professional to have a giant olive bush floating past in the background along with a scrawny, hot and bothered boyfriend cursing the trees and rueing the day he ever bought them.

I eventually got them to the outdoor terrace and although it was a lot of faff and effort, my goodness did I feel good once they were there. I treated myself to a hard-earned cider and admired my new babies.

It was incredible how they made the outdoor space feel totally different and calmer. If it wasn't for the occasional waft of chicken nuggets from the nearby McDonald's and the constant beeping and shouting by angry motorists on the roundabout below, then I would have felt like I was sunning it up on a lounger in Mykonos . . . well, maybe not Mykonos, but very close to it. The Costa del Roundabout?

Ways to create a gorgeous outdoor space – without breaking the bank

Plant colourful perennials such as geraniums. They will keep coming back year after year and you've only paid for (and planted) them once. Plant them in the spring so they have two seasons of warmth in which to establish and grow before the colder weather sets in.

1. Solar-powered outdoor fairy lights can transform a space into a twinkly oasis.

2. If short on space, create your own vertical garden by hanging boxes on hooks and planting violas and lobelias for colour. You can also plant things like strawberries, lettuce and spinach.

3. Make a vegetable garden from kitchen scraps. The root bases of spring onions and celery are great for this.

4. Lay down an outdoor rug to make any space feel a bit more stylish.

5. Put a pop of colour in by giving a fence a lick of bright paint. Make sure you prep it correctly first with a pressure wash and a coat of primer. And check the weather forecast! It's pointless doing this in the rain.

6. Go forth and multiply! Divide up your perennials by gently digging up the clumps, separating the root ball into two or three sections and replanting apart. It's really easy to do and also helps keep the plants robust and healthy.

7. Upcycling. Sometimes bits of old unwanted junk to some people could be perfect for transforming into a planter or windchime or anything else. Pinterest has some great examples of some of the amazing things you can do with old bits and pieces and it's really satisfying when someone asks, 'Oooh, where did you get that from?' to which you reply in a smug manner: 'I made it myself.'

The importance of outdoor space

After the arrival of the olive trees I wanted to chase that dopamine hit of satisfaction from garden improvement and so when retail reopened, I would drag Dianne along to any garden centre within a certain radius to us. Partly because in those times that's what counted as a fun day out, but also because I wanted to add more to these outside areas we had in our London flat.

It didn't get off to the smoothest of starts and I may have bought some plants who took to their new home so badly that they decided they'd be better off dead than live the rest of their lives with the constant aroma of chicken McNuggets and feeling intimidated by the giant olive trees.

RIP to those early plants. They did not die in vain because they paved the way and sacrificed themselves so I could learn why this happened and have a deeper understanding of what works best in different areas.

After many days and many phone calls to Mum asking her what the different John Innes soils meant, I had created a small but satisfying urban garden which I strongly believe helped keep us sane when the world was in dark times.

I would sit in my little calm green patch and feel relaxed and safe, but it would also make me reflect on all the people who weren't fortunate enough to have any outdoor space at all, especially during lockdown. I had a few friends who lived in neighbouring apartments in the same development as us who experienced it this way and they really struggled.

Like most species, we work best when we're free range. Health experts from the universities of the Highlands and Islands and Aberdeen surveyed around

3,000 people in Scotland across June and July in 2020 and found that people who did not have gardens or patios experienced greater mental health challenges than those who did.

But I've also seen great examples of people with little to no outdoor space getting creative. Vertical gardens are becoming more and more popular. Not only do they tick the box of taking up hardly any space, but they are also good for the environment, help purify the air and give you that responsibility of looking after plants. Trust me, it's such a good feeling when you watch them grow.

You don't need to break the bank to make one either. Take a wooden pallet, turn it on its side, stick a few potted plants in there and boom! You have yourself one vertical garden, my friend.

If you know what you want to achieve with the space you have, this is when social media can actually come into its own and be both productive and inspiring. Pinterest, Instagram, YouTube and gardening blogs can be great for this – the internet holds all the answers to the nichest of garden questions.

Even for those of us who live in busy cities and don't have lots of space, there are still plenty of ways to tempt wildlife into your midst. Did you know that different seeds in bird feeders attract different species? Niger seeds are great for attracting goldfinches and they are such beautiful birds it feels like an honour when they grace you with their presence.

You can attract nature into your space wherever you are. And if you're really desperate to make friends with wildlife, try not taking the bins out for a couple of weeks.

Actually, that's terrible advice, don't do that. Promise me you won't do that.

How to use different foods to attract wild birds to your outdoor space

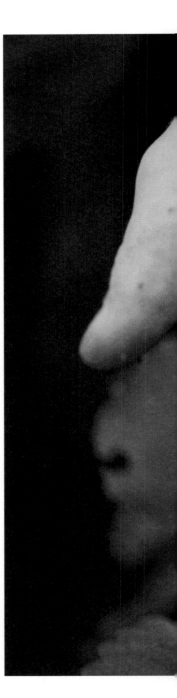

Crushed peanuts (must not be salted or dry roasted)
Robins, dunnocks and wrens

Mealworms
Blue tits, pied wagtails, blackbirds, thrushes

Small seeds
Sparrows, finches

Sunflower seeds
Tits, finches, siskins

Niger seeds
Goldfinches, sparrows, great spotted woodpeckers

Grandad's garden

I've picked up a lot of what I know from observing my parents and being given chores around the garden (watering the lawn in the summer was my domain) and being able to discern a weed from Mum's prize dahlias.

Mum still spends time working on her garden or checking her vegetables in the greenhouse, and everything she knows was passed down by my grandad who grew up on a farm in Somerset. And I'm sure he learnt from his mother and father and so on and so forth.

My grandad, Richard Chapman, was a very special figure in my life. He was an extremely creative man and one of his outlets was his garden. Whenever we used to visit our grandparents, I could never understand how their lawn was always so pristine. It was almost as though every blade of grass had been hand-placed.

The borders were all bursting with colour and then there was Grandad's vegetable patch where he grew tomatoes, runner beans and, hands down, the world's best new potatoes.

Along with his family, his garden was his pride and joy, and if he wasn't working on his own, he would be round our house helping us with ours, pruning away and passing down the knowledge.

I did notice that the further back this knowledge went, the more folklore-ish it became – it seemed that back in the olden days everything was taught via the medium of rhyme. My mum also told me that when she was a child, she remembers my grandad stopping the car to scoop up horse poo from the road and putting it in the back to take home to sprinkle on the roses.

This is a story I can fully believe and it's a practice I'll at least consider replicating next time I'm out on a walk and come across a big steamy horse poo.

Sadly, my grandad passed away in September 2021. The funeral was a beautiful celebration of his life with family and close friends who all shared fond memories of this wonderful man.

In true Grandad style, the flowers on the coffin were mixed with tomatoes and runner beans which I thought was exactly what he would have loved. After the ceremony we were all given a small brown paper sachet with a piece of straw-like string tied around it in a little bow and the words printed in beautiful script: *'All you need to forget me not is love, water and sunshine.'*

Inside was a handful of forget-me-not seeds. Along with homegrown tomatoes, green beans and new potatoes, I will make sure that my future garden space has these little flowers planted so I'm always reminded of my grandad.

I want to feel like he is with me whenever I am working away, keeping the weeds at bay or trying to grow vegetables just like he used to, and I'll imagine him shaking his head chuckling to himself and saying: 'Joe's got a lot to learn in this garden . . . he's certainly got his work cut out!'

And he would not be wrong. After moving to this new space and spending a good amount of time here, I've seen how the seasons come and go through this garden and the changes they bring. What really surprised me was that for the last seven years of being in London I had completely forgotten how the different seasons affect the spaces around you.

Living in a busy concrete jungle for all that time, I'd only notice that it got colder in autumn and winter and that it would generally be miserable. And then in spring and summer it would usually still be rainy and miserable but you might get lucky and have a few nice weeks of glorious sunshine.

But since moving to the countryside, I've been pleasantly surprised to find that in early February at the bottom of our sloped garden there are these rogue green shoots which pop out of the cold ground left, right and centre.

I had no idea what they were at first and so, of course, I called my mum to ask if they were supposed to be there.

'They're snowdrops and daffodils, darling,' she explained to me.

Snowdrops! Daffodils! Growing in our garden and we didn't even need to plant them or look after them! It was free nature!

'And guess what,' added Mum, 'they'll most likely come back year after year.'

I couldn't believe it. Not only did it serve as a brilliant backdrop for an impromptu photoshoot for Dianne's Instagram, they would also return next year, too!

In fact, that reminds me of the one time I've seen my mum get confrontational. As a kid, I remember hearing her shouting at someone from her bedroom window one Sunday morning. Now, I hadn't done anything wrong (nothing since the last time I was sent to my room anyway) and my sister was always good as gold, so who on earth was Mum yelling at?

I hurried up the stairs to see what all the hysteria was about and to my surprise there was Mum leaning out the window shaking her fist at a young couple who had pulled over on the side of the road and were picking her daffs from the verge outside our house.

'OI! I'VE PLANTED THOSE! GET AWAY FROM MY DAFFODILS, YOU YOUNG RAPSCALLIONS!' is not what she said, but it was something along those lines. I just wanted to add in the word 'rapscallions' for my own personal enjoyment.

In seven years of living in London, the only times I saw daffodils were in supermarkets, and I had completely forgotten that gardens and outdoor spaces are always changing as the seasons come and go.

We watched so many other changes over the next few months. Plants we had assumed were mere green bushes started to bloom with colour.

'Ah, we can't get rid of that now, Dianne! It's one of those bushes that goes a lovely pinky purple colour,' I'd say very knowledgeably while making a mental note in the new gardening section of my brain.

Don't be daunted by the prospect of what, when and where to plant in the garden. I'm still very much a gardening novice and am learning all the time, and that is all part of the fun and satisfaction I get from it! Plus, so often with gardening it isn't a case of hard and fast rules; it's about trying things gently at first, seeing what works, and getting to know what suits your indoor plants or outdoor space.

How to plan your garden

Find the right month for planting:

January–February – you can get your summer bedding flowers going from seed now (turn to page 172 for some step-by-step guidance on this), as long as you have somewhere warm to house them until they're ready to go into the ground.

May – if you're planting seedlings for flowering from late June onwards, now's the time.

October – the perfect time to get your spring bulbs in the ground. That's your daffodils, crocuses and snowdrops. Tulips can generally wait until November, but the smaller bulbs should be in while the earth is still warm from the autumn weather.

Track the sun in your outdoor space before planting – some plants and flowers such as foxgloves, begonia and fuchsia will fare better in the shade, whereas others, such as petunia, marigolds and geraniums prefer to bask in the sunshine.

Plan your borders carefully by putting the taller guys at the back and make sure you plant everything with enough space in between – the label or the info on the packet will tell you how far apart they need to be from each other in order to have room to bloom.

Some flowers are easier to grow and maintain than others – if you're a beginner, these guys are a great place to start.

Marigolds

These beauties are quick growers, especially if they're planted in plenty of sun.

Plant: May–June

Sweet peas

These colourful climbers look great and smell even better and don't need much space. They are also fantastic for cutting.

Plant: Late May

Sunflowers

Plant from seed and watch them shoot up throughout the summer and keep on going well into autumn.

Plant: April

Geraniums

These guys never let you down. Such stoicism! And more colours to choose from than you can shake a stick at.

Plant: May

Pansies

A classic in any garden, they are the gift that keeps on giving if you deadhead them often enough. You can get summer and winter varieties to have colour all year round.

Plant: Summer pansies, May. Winter pansies, September–October

If you're growing veg, some make better companions than others, so plan what goes where ahead of planting. For instance, carrots grow well with lettuce, cabbage and tomatoes. Most veg grow in a sunny spot but also be mindful that they will need shelter from strong winds.

Prune regularly and you will reap the benefits of fuller flowers for longer.

Beware of garden pests like slugs. They will do their level best to destroy all your hard work. There are lots of tips and tricks for keeping them at bay and it's worth trying as many as possible. A container of beer in the flower bed can lure them before they fall in and get stuck. Crushed eggshells or pine needles can help form a barrier around your plants which can act as a slug deterrent. And plants such as fennel and rosemary can also give off a scent which drives them away. Good luck!

Raising and then planting from seed before transferring to the ground is a much more cost-effective way of gardening than buying ready-grown seedlings from the garden centre. And the job satisfaction when it goes right is immense!

Raising

Find the perfect spot where your little friends are going to be warm and dry during the winter months until it's time to put them in the ground. The best temperature for them is 18–20 degrees Celsius.

* Your containers should have drainage holes and a depth of 5–6 cm. Have a rummage through your recycling because you can make your containers from old ice cream or butter tubs, takeaway boxes or milk cartons!

* Fill your containers almost to the brim with soil.

* Sow your seeds carefully, leaving enough space around each one.

* Gently sieve some more soil on top.

* Label them so you don't forget what's what!

* Give them a good drink with a spray bottle of water.

* Leave them to germinate in their temporary home and water regularly to keep the soil moist.

Planting

* Make sure the seedling is ready to transfer to the ground – if it has two or three leaves it should be about time, and it should be around late May.

* They should be very well watered before you lift them out of their containers.

* Dig a hole a little wider and deeper than the pot and gently lift out your plant and place it in the hole.

* Fill in the space around it with soil and water. Tend to them with love.

Learning on the job

I spent a lot of 2021 learning, remembering the rhymes and Pinteresting to help mould our outdoor space into exactly what we want it to become. I would take regular trips to the local garden centre and browse the bulbs and seeds section like a child would with pick n mix. But instead of fizzy cola bottles and foamy shrimps and bananas, it was sunflower seeds and lavender plants.

The sunflowers were my pride and joy of 2021. There was a local contest going on in our village to see who could grow the most impressive sunflower. It was my first time growing anything like this and so I learnt the hard way that growing sunflowers in a pot will only allow the plants to grow so tall before you have to re-home them in the earth and just cross your fingers and toes that the rabbits don't eat them.

Sadly, I missed the end of the competition, but in early October, I was the only person in my whole village who had sunflowers still in full bloom. They were late bloomers! Just like their dad!

In the summer months I really got into lavender and having pots of plants on the decking that gave off a lovely smell. Lavender is very calming and also great for helping you wind down and have a good sleep.

The other plant that became my favourite of the year was the *Artemisia abrotanum*, otherwise known as the garden sagebrush. The reason this was such a hit was because it has the aroma of cola! Every person that comes to visit us has to take on 'Joe's garden smell test' and try and guess what they can smell from this plant.

I don't know why, but I always get a great kick out of showing visitors this guy!

I've also been growing my collection of gardening tools. I got my first strimmer to tackle the lethal stinging nettles which absolutely took over our garden in the summer. After watching strimmer reviews on YouTube which put my tailored algorithm of recommended videos completely out of whack for a good month or two afterwards, I finally found the bit of kit I needed to take on the job myself.

It probably would have been a much smarter move for me to use all the time put into waging war on the stingers into something more productive work-wise. But for me, this was exactly what I needed to relax my busy brain and give myself a manual labour task that would release those oh-so important endorphins and a sense of self-sufficiency.

I've enjoyed sharing my garden escapades on social media, but like everything on there, it's come with complications. No sooner had I done my research on which strimmer to get, gone to the agricultural machinery shop to buy the blimming thing and got all the modern-day protection on (which they definitely wouldn't have had back in the old days), my phone buzzes and it's a message from my nan, who had seen my posts showing what I was about to do, and replied with: 'But butterflies love stinging nettles!'

To make it even worse, as I looked up from the message, a single butterfly landed on one of the nettles and did what butterflies do, I guess, and showed off its beautiful wings. I couldn't possibly hack them all down after that, could I?

I decided to compromise and find a middle ground. Rather than obliterating every stinger in sight with my new shiny destroying machine, I carefully strimmed a pathway, wide enough for a human to easily walk through without ending up with itchy lumps around their ankles but also leaving plenty for the butterflies to enjoy.

At this point you might think: 'Hey, that must be great using social media to help you with advice and make decisions!'

And yes, I champion this . . . to a point. It's so great that we have these mini-computers in our pockets that we can just whip out at any decision-making moment and get the advice we want to reassure ourselves we're doing the right thing.

But it can also be an absolute nightmare. I learnt very quickly in my career online that the bigger your audience grows, the harder it is to please everyone. Whatever I post, say or produce is not going to be everyone's cup of tea.

It was quite disheartening at first (I've already told you I'm a natural people-pleaser), because I started my YouTube channel and Instagram and other platforms purely to entertain anyone who stumbled across my content.

But growth means attracting an audience with lots of people who have strong opinions and people with strong opinions sure do love to share 'em.

If I ever ask for advice on social media – it might be gardening, DIY, even evening skincare routines – it's always been fascinating to see the replies. Everyone has such contrasting theories and they all swear that theirs is correct.

I've come to realize that the road I'm on is a journey. It's not a straight road, it's full of bends and obstacles, and any decision I make or turning I take isn't going to be the 'correct' one in everyone's eyes.

It's what makes us human though. We are all different in our own beautiful way and that should be celebrated, not changed.

So many people messaged me after I opted to save a load of nettles for the sake of the butterflies to tell me I was 'stupid' or even 'insane' to keep the weeds growing in the garden. I appreciate their input, but I always listen to my nan and so the butterflies win, soz.

I know that doing the job I do invites the world and his wife to offer up their version of how they would do things. But at the end of the day, whether it's stinging nettles or deciding when to get your fat balls out for the birds (this is not, I repeat NOT, an intended innuendo), it comes down to what I want to do and how I want to live my life.

I can take advice on board, but ultimately, it's me and only me calling the shots. This sense of responsibility is quite scary but also so empowering, and being able to make decisions for yourself without needing validation from strangers feels very freeing.

And when I'm out in the garden and I see the butterflies having a wild party around those nettles, the online shouting shrinks away to insignificance. You can always rely on nature to put what matters – what really matters – into perspective.

Chapter 5

BRINGING THE OUTSIDE IN

As a 'congratuwelldone' for staying with me and making it all the way to chapter five, I'm going to let you into a little behind-the-scenes secret.

To make sure this book sees the light of publication day, I had to get myself into a good routine. It's sad to say that my relationship with routine has been lacking ever since the day I put down my Leggett. Don't panic, a Leggett isn't a breed of dog (at least I don't think it is). It's a roof thatcher's favourite bit of kit and is used for tapping the freshly laid bundles of straw on the roof, keeping it all uniform and pretty.

I've struggled to keep a good routine with the work I do post-thatching as it's very 'day by day' and I seem to have stretched myself across a lot of different interests which, in turn, have led to more great work opportunities.

Picture one of those people who do that whole one-man-band kind of thing wearing a musical contraption so when they move a body part it plays an instrument. That's how I feel sometimes.

So, when I committed to writing my very own book *and* illustrating it, I knew I would have to get some proper structure put in place to keep everyone happy, including myself.

On my writing days I'd usually sit down at a certain time in a certain spot with a certain 'concentration playlist' keeping me, well, concentrated. I would then deliver the finished chapter the next day, like a good boy. Although – and here comes the much anticipated behind-the-scenes secret – this chapter is unfortunately going to break that routine and won't be delivered on time. And the reason for this . . . is houseplants.

I wanted to talk to you about bringing the outside indoors and the weird way in which my mind works – and I don't know if this is because of the way I was brought up, my star sign (Virgo – industrious, methodical and practical) or perhaps I was a Swiss cheese plant in a former life – but my conscience kicked in as soon as I sat down to write this chapter and it steadfastly refused to let me write a single word until I had done the rounds and watered every little green member of the family in our home.

I just didn't have it in me to write/bitch about them before giving them a drink and a gentle leaf dusting. It would have felt like I was going behind their backs, if plants indeed have backs, that is.

So I'm writing this chapter now a lot later than I'd have liked to, but with a clear conscience knowing that the plants around me are happy. Phew!

The benefits of indoor gardening

1. Studies have shown that indoor plants can help reduce stress and lower blood pressure.

2. According to the Royal Horticultural Society, indoor plants can boost mood and be good for mental wellbeing.

3. Adding plants to a work environment can increase productivity.

4. In hospital settings they were shown to increase pain tolerance.

5. Indoor plants can improve the air quality by eliminating pollutants.

Why we've gone potty for plants

I'm by no means alone in my houseplant obsession. It's boom time for plant culture, which is a craze growing quicker than the Swiss cheese twins after a pint of water.

Online plant store Patch Plants reported a sales hike of 500 per cent during the pandemic. And the Royal Horticultural Society said there had been a 533 per cent increase in the number of eighteen- to twenty-four-year-olds visiting its website over that time.

Social media, as ever, has played a major part in this, and we are seeing the rise of the 'plantfluencer'. That's right, there are plenty of Instagram accounts out there made by proud plant owners showing off their potted pals and the wonderful green aesthetic of their indoor plants.

And it seems that it's the Millennials and Gen Zs – the generations who have grown up online – who are fronting this movement. Perhaps it's the trend for settling down later in life and delaying the expense of having children playing a part in the increase. Plant babies as opposed to real babies? Maybe.

Tending to needy houseplants could also be offering the younger generations a much-needed antidote to the fast-paced, ever-changing world of social media. We, as humans, thrive off connection and the idea of nurturing, whether that's another human, pet or plant.

Apparently, they can even give us physical health benefits, such as reduced blood pressure and reduced fatigue.

And according to my girlfriend, she gets many health benefits from hacking up my beloved aloe vera. And bizarrely, she's absolutely on the money – more on this later.

Favourite houseplants

It's wrong to have favourite children, but I can't help it. Here are my top five houseplants:

Snake plant – reliable, slick, tough

The best thing about these guys is that they are pretty much indestructible! They're so low maintenance, you really only need to water them once or twice a month. Even less during the winter months. They're not too bothered about location either and they're known for being pretty effective air purifiers. In short, there's an awful lot to love about them.

Monstera – show-off, adventurous, excitable

This is another very beginner-friendly houseplant but be warned – they can take on a life of their own very quickly! Monsteras or cheese plants like bright, indirect sunlight and moist soil, so make sure they're watered around once a week. Overwatering will lead to yellow leaves. They love humidity and will appreciate a misting every other day.

Aloe vera – intimidating, soothing, alien

These fellas store water in their leaves and so really don't need to be watered all that often. And not at all during the winter months. A bright spot on a windowsill is the perfect location for an aloe, and to make use of its healing qualities, cut away the leaf at the base and rub the sap directly on to the affected skin.

String of pearls – Instafamous, beautiful, the glue that holds a plant collection together

Such a stoic plant and needs very little care. Water about once a month during the winter and once every couple of weeks during the warmer months. Pruning might be necessary every so often – just trim any dead pearls and stems and this will promote healthier, fuller growth.

Areca palm – tropical, gets you in the holiday mood, showpiece

A bit more effort is required with this one but it's definitely worth it. They need bright but indirect sunlight and just the right amount of watering. Too much or too little and they'll punish you – the soil should be permanently moist but never soaked through. Mist the leaves a few times a week and bear in mind it will probably need repotting every couple of years.

My first foray into houseplanting

I reckon my earliest experience of indoor plants would have been as a five- or six-year-old and (as I'm sure many of you will relate to) came with the Venus flytrap!

'Wait, so this plant has a mouth and fangs and eats things?' I asked as a wide-eyed youngster, on seeing this alien-like plant for the first time at a garden centre. I was absolutely fascinated by these plants and since they are always portrayed as terrifying green and purple killing machines (they definitely need to work on their PR), I was desperate to have some in my room to threaten my sister if she was ever annoying me.

Sadly, I don't believe I ever owned my own Venus flytrap. And this was perhaps because I quickly moved on to a much bigger and more badass houseplant. The cactus.

I bought my very first cactus at a boot sale of all places. I can't remember how much for, but it was a boot sale so it definitely would have been a bargain compared to what you would pay nowadays. It even came with its own pot and although it was small in stature, I could see its potential.

The cactus was a cool plant to have in your bedroom as a child. It had that element of danger to it and went splendidly with the lime-green paint on my walls.

It took pride of place on my south-facing windowsill, soaking up the sunlight and doing what cacti do best . . . just being a cactus. Although it didn't do much else other than look cool, I still have fond memories thinking back to that little green spiky friend of mine. I was instructed to water it just once in a blue moon and it would stay alive. Which it did – he lasted almost all my childhood.

You can probably tell by now that I cling on to very detailed and obscure memories from childhood, many of which have shaped me into the person I am today.

A lot of these memories are lovely and positive, but unfortunately there are some which haunt me to this day, and every now and then my mind likes to throw them back up from the depths to remind me of all the times I've embarrassed myself in public or not spoken up when I should have, or that even though I'm lucky enough to be writing a fancy book about growth, I still did that horrible thing to my friend back in the early 2000s.

Thanks, brain.

It happened in my bedroom right before the summer holidays in 2001 (I know this because it was a hot day and the cactus was absolutely loving it) and my best mate in primary school, Jordan, came over to play.

We were playing about in my room and both going through a 'wrestling phase'. Even though they clearly state at the start of the wrestling shows 'DO NOT TRY THIS AT HOME!', when you're in your own room you think it's highly unlikely that The Undertaker is going to burst through your bedroom door and chokeslam you through the floor into the kitchen sink below (ahhh, maybe that's why that hole was there in the house before it was renovated!) for attempting it at home.

Anyway, the bedroom wrestling match escalated, and I ended up pushing Jordan and he fell back towards the windowsill where my boot sale cactus was living his best life and you can guess what happened next.

I was horrified by what I had done and rushed to help pull the cactus prickles out of my best mate's hand as he looked down in blind panic.

Even though I was eleven at the time, that memory has stayed with me and every now and then comes back to just give me a friendly reminder to not be a prick to my friends (pun intended).

Thankfully, both Jordan and the cactus survived. But unfortunately, as I entered my teenage years, I started to care less and less for that poor cactus. Picture that montage in *Toy Story* when Andy starts to ignore Woody in favour of becoming a Buzz Lightyear fanboy. That was what it was like except Woody was the cactus and *Warhammer* was my Buzz Lightyear.

Nevertheless, the cactus stood firm and managed to live on for most of my teens, but it eventually got to the stage where it looked like an ice mummy's frostbitten finger. And by the time I got off my lazy teenage arse to try and revive it, it was too late.

RIP cactus. Some will say you were too good for my windowsill. Too good for this cruel world even. And they would be right. You will forever be in my heart, and immortalized in this chapter.

How to make your own terrarium

Terrariums or bottle gardens were a big trend back in the 70s and they're currently enjoying a revival. Quite right, too! They're a great way to bring nature indoors, they look really cool and they're super easy to make from scratch.

What you'll need:

1. A glass container (could be an old jam jar if you're starting really dinky, a larger cookie jar or a goldfish bowl)

2. Some small pebbles for drainage

3. Activated charcoal (you can get this at your garden centre)

4. Potting soil

5. A chopstick or long spoon

6. Plants, obvs (some good starters for closed terrariums include the spider plant, ivy, moss, peperomia and miniature ferns)

7. Start by layering your pebbles in the bottom of the container, about 2 cm deep, and then scatter the charcoal across.

8. Next, put in the soil making sure it's deep enough for the plants' roots to be comfortable. Using your chopstick or spoon, make a hole in the middle of the soil and place your plant gently into it. You can add more than one plant if you have a big enough container.

9. Add a few more pebbles on top of the soil and you're done!

10. Tropical plants are better off in humid conditions so best to keep a lid on these guys. It's fine to leave the top open for succulents and cacti.

11. You can add decorations such as moss or figurines or shells. Get creative!

12. Check the soil every few weeks and give it a little drink if it's dry. And if you've got a lid, take it off once a month to avoid condensation and help increase airflow.

Becoming a plant parent

I first took on full-blown plant responsibility when I moved into my own flat in London as a young adult. The flat was unfurnished and I had no furniture. I didn't even have curtains for the first month of living there so I slept in an actual wardrobe.

Now, does that sound like the sort of young adult that has their shit together and is ready to take on more responsibility and look after other living things? Yikes.

After slowly learning how to make a modern, white-walled flat look 'homely' I discovered that there was a vital piece of the puzzle missing. So I took a trip to my local garden centre, or nursery. I think it's funny that they call it a nursery; it's like they're subtly reminding you that you're about to take responsibility for another life . . . but I digress.

So, I walked around the nursery and must admit, I got a bit too into it. So many different sizes and types of plant! I felt a bit like a houseplant Noah trying to cram two of every breed into my ark (or, rather, my small trolley).

I took it to the till, super excited about becoming a plant daddy ready to oxygenate his flat and slowly turn it into a green paradise.

'That will be £400, please,' said the smiley lady behind the till. 'Will you need help carrying them to the car?'

'Well, for £400 I expect them all to be delivered individually by an UberLUX!' is what I didn't say.

Instead, I smiled back and, very Britishly, said: 'No, it's fine. I can manage, thank you.'

I never knew these things were so pricey! Then again, I don't have real life children yet and I've heard that they're not exactly cheap either . . .

I took my new family back to the flat and took the register. We had the twins, who were two Swiss cheese plants or monsteras. These two were magnificent. They're climbers and they grew so quickly in my bathroom that you could almost watch it happening in real time.

If they were human, they would be the show performers that like to leave you on the edge of your seat, a bit like Penn and Teller. There would be times where they'd look really worse for wear and I thought I'd lost them and then, BOOM! A good watering and bit of sunlight and not only had they risen from the brink of death but they'd almost doubled in size!

I also had an eight-foot monstera which I ended up just calling Lurch after the tall manservant from *The Addams Family*. This giant was my showpiece and also the reason I nearly caused a car crash as people slowed down to see him poking out the sunroof of my mum's Mini Cooper.

I had a few string of pearls which are the best ones for having on a ledge and hanging down, instantly making your indoor space look ten times cooler. If these plants were human, they would be the super chilled hippy dudes who just hang out all day admiring the world around them.

I love aloe vera plants, they're a personal favourite of mine. Mainly because I feel so sorry for them, just sitting there in their pots minding their own business when all of a sudden, my girlfriend comes along and cuts a chunk off to put on her skin!

Turns out it's OK to do and is good for your skin, especially if you're sunburnt. But the look of horror on my face when she attacked my treasured aloe vera for the first time was something to behold, and I think it was at that moment that I realized that I'd become quite the protective houseplant father.

Another of my favourites is the snake plant. Cool name and just an all-round solid plant to have about the place. The snake plant doesn't complain, it doesn't whinge or moan, it just gets on with life and is fine with that.

If a snake plant was a human, it would be like Arnie in *Terminator 2*. Snake plant doesn't need no praise or fuss, it knows what its purpose is and just gets the job done. This plant is also known as 'mother-in-law's tongue' due to its long, sharp leaves, which is funny because one thing that Dianne's mum Rina and I instantly bonded over was our love of gardening and houseplants.

I know she'll be reading this, so I want to let you know, Rina, that I will always, always refer to it as a snake plant.

Other plants in my brood that deserve an honourable mention are the bamboo palm, corn plant, money tree, heart-leaf philodendron and also a final shout out to all the little succulents, the forgotten heroes in my plant family, mainly because after all these years of being a plant dad, I still can't work out what they are.

And lastly, the terrariums! I have a few scattered out around the house (all were gifts from friends or people I have worked with) and I love them because they're like their own little ecosystems which also makes me think a bit too deep about stuff like: 'What if Planet Earth is just a big terrarium?' and I guess in a weird way it kind of is, right?

How not to kill your houseplants

1. Regular misting will keep leaves clean and maintain the plant's humidity (although don't do this with cacti or succulents as they generally prefer to be dry).

2. Don't be tempted to over-water. Only give your plants a drink when the top 2 cm of soil is dry – check once or twice a week.

3. Use room temperature water to feed them.

4. Choose an appropriate-sized pot for your plant (your garden centre can advise you on this) and line the bottom with stones or lava rocks which will provide crevices for the water to drain into.

5. Any dead leaves, cut from the base using sharp scissors.

6. Avoid placing them where they will have direct sunlight.

7. I use my mum's potting mix for my houseplants and it is SO good. Use houseplant potting mix from your local garden centre, or if you're feeling more adventurous, you can add fir bark, for aeration and good drainage, and it helps the roots by having something to grow around. You can add perlite (or vermiculite) for airy soil and it prevents root rot.

Plant rants

For the few of you hoping this book would have some major tea spilling or 'dragging', which I think means to berate or slander without the person knowing, you're not going to be disappointed.

Well, you probably will be, because I'm going to trash-talk the houseplants that I've just never gotten on with.

First up, I'm sorry to say it, the rubber plant. I know, I know, you're probably now shouting at this book and threatening to burn it or tear this page out, but hang on and let me explain.

I want to like this plant so much, but I have a bit of a *Groundhog Day* experience as I seem to repeat the same disastrous cycle with it again and again, forgetting to learn from my mistakes every time. Notice how I said 'my' mistakes there. I would love nothing more than to put at least part of the blame on the rubber plant itself, but I will be the bigger person in this.

I've owned five or six of these bad boys in my life. And every one of them has suffered the same fate and I STILL DON'T KNOW WHY!

For a so-called beginner plant, it's way too fussy for me. It wants sunlight but not direct sunlight, it wants watering twice a week and moisture in the soil but not too much moisture and not too little, also let the top of the soil dry first before watering again . . . aaarrgh!! Talk about precious! It just wants too much from me!

I also found out that it's poisonous to pets and humans if it's eaten, not that I've ever wanted to eat one because I can't keep one alive long enough to do so.

It seems to be the go-to plant for people to give me for birthdays, or social gatherings as a thank you. 'No, no, thank *you* for inadvertently bringing back all the traumatic memories of past attempts to keep them alive!'

Note to friends and family, I appreciate the thought but please, for the love of all things botanical, stop buying me rubber plants.

Another plant that unfortunately falls into this easy gift category is the rattlesnake. It pains me to even write these words because I adore this guy. It's probably in my top three visually pleasing houseplants. (Yes, I do have a list of most visually pleasing houseplants, and what of it?) But once again, I just can't for the life of me seem to keep them alive! This one needs constantly damp soil but cannot – I repeat CANNOT – be left in too much water otherwise those pretty leaves? Yeah, they won't be there in a few days' time.

What makes it even worse is that it's got the word snake in its name which just serves to remind me of how robust the snake plant is, just sitting there being perfect, never making a fuss. And then you've got its wimpy cousin the rattlesnake over there which, if it drinks too much, literally melts.

Trust me when I say the positives of having houseplants massively outweigh any negatives. Yes, they can be quite pricey in some places, and some will die within a week and you'll ask yourself 'Why did I bother?', but taking on that responsibility and watching these things grow because of the love and care you give them gives you a really good feeling. They do so much more than merely improve the look of your living space.

As well as lowering stress, increasing calm and encouraging both physiological and psychological relaxation, houseplants mean that no matter where we live, we can all have nature in our homes.

Nurturing them becomes routine and provides some structure which, as I mentioned at the beginning of this chapter, is something I've discovered is quite important for me.

You do get a bit attached to your little green buddies. When moving from London to the countryside, we hired a removal company (by the end of moving day we were a lot less sure that they were in fact a removal company, but that's another story for another day) to take all our belongings to the new house.

I don't really have valuable items other than, I guess, camera equipment and other YouTubey type things, but it was the houseplants I was most nervous about handing over to the removal guys who, let's face it, probably couldn't care less.

They'd take one look at the brown, pathetic stump in a pot and think: 'Is that shrivelled up, dead thing supposed to be a rubber plant?'

I could imagine all the plants in the van as they made the journey from London to Sussex. The string of pearls would have been just chilling there saying (in plant voices): 'Let's just all chill out, guys, everything's going to be mellow, duuuude', the monstera twins would have been climbing on and spreading across all the boxes and the snake plant would have been minding its own business, completely unfazed by the chaos of the aloe vera losing a limb and the removal men meandering around London, hitting every pothole in sight.

However, you'll be pleased to know the plants did make it to the new house in one piece and, like me and Dianne, have settled there very well. The comfort and sense of grounding they bring is immeasurable and I'm not ashamed to admit that I now get excited to visit the garden centre. I wonder how many houseplants I can give a new home to before people start raising eyebrows . . .

They really do add a sense of cosiness and calm to the house and mean we are cocooned in nature at all times in return for minimal effort. What's not to love?

Chapter 6

THE POWER OF AWE & LIVING FOR NOW

Have you ever witnessed a thing of beauty or natural event that was so breath-taking you actually forgot to whip out your phone to capture it and post online? And so now your friends don't believe you saw it and think you make stuff up to try and impress people so they've cast you out of the group for telling porkies?

I feel lucky enough to say that I have been in quite a few situations where I've witnessed something amazing in nature and forgotten to capture it. You may be thinking: 'Why is it lucky to not capture the moment and share it online? You never know, Joe, you could potentially get the big call up from *National Geographic* if it gets enough likes and shares.'

Well, I very much doubt that but also, I've become really aware of the importance of living in the moment and finding that perfect balance of what to share and what to just enjoy for myself.

For example, walking along the cliff tops of the Jurassic coast and watching the powerful waves smashing into the ancient cliff face made me feel very present.

It's a tricky situation for me as part of what I've done for the last ten years is to share my life online, but I've developed a system over time of how to do that and still feel like I'm doing it for me.

I'm a highly skilled Draft Saver. Fun fact about us Draft Savers – we're a rare breed and very capable of capturing great memories via photo, video, or even gif! But rather than missing out on the rest of that moment by racking our brains for the best possible caption or leaving the situation completely to find a signal so we can get our post or POV up before our friends do, Draft Savers will save what we captured, yes, you guessed it, into our drafts so we can focus on the now.

Then, after we've enjoyed time with the people around us, creating memories and being present, we'll find a quiet place and some down time (usually alone)

to look back through the photos and videos we took, apply whatever filters are needed and clever captions, and that is that.

Now that I'm a fully-fledged Draft Saver, it's brought more joy into what's actually there in front of me, be that relationships and experiences with friends, or even just going out for a walk in nature and enjoying and appreciating my surroundings.

Nature is just the most mind-boggling thing and no matter how much we can learn about it and admire it from a Google search or a Pinterest board, seeing and experiencing some of the wonderful landscapes we have in this world can really have a positive impact on us.

How awe can be . . . awesome

In that vein, I've been reading about the power of awe and how experiencing the feeling of being completely blown away by the wonder of nature can be really beneficial to our mental wellbeing. It's definitely not something you can feel while filming it on your phone, by the way. How can you lose yourself in the moment if you're witnessing it through a screen while trying to make sure you've lined up the camera at the perfect angle? Are you truly enjoying and taking in what's happening in front of you if you're faffing about with your phone and thinking about how many 'likes' it's going to get?

I wanted to Google what the actual definition of awe was as I knew I had felt it before, on many occasions, but putting it into words is quite tricky. And so for everyone's sake . . .

Awe – *a feeling of reverential respect mixed with fear or wonder.*

As you can imagine, this brought up further questions in my mind like: 'When did I first feel awe? When did I last feel awe? What's the most awe I've ever felt? And what's it measured in exactly?'

And also: 'What does reverential mean?'

Experts say that if you're feeling down, then you might need to experience more awe in your life. According to psychologists Dacher Keltner and Jonathan Haidt, who have done a lot of research into this whole concept, the emotion of awe 'can equally be elicited by religious as secular phenomena, such as nature, panoramic views, and works of art'.

They describe awe as the feeling of wonder, or the emotional response experienced when faced with something vaster than yourself (whether that vastness is real or perceived) and beyond understanding.

Awe-some stuff.

It's made me think back and realize that I've felt awe throughout my life, a lot more than I initially thought. Going on a plane for the first time, I cried my eyes out and actually turned around on the tarmac and tried to run back to the safety of the airport.

My dad had to run after me, scoop me up and carry me up the stairs, otherwise we'd never have made it to Portugal and experienced that secret beach with beautiful gold sands. Or that lookout point to the Atlantic Ocean and the terrifying cliff drop. That intense mix of fear and surprise was probably awe too.

After take-off, the popping of ears and more tears, we broke through the cloud to be met with the open expanse of blue sky. I had just figured out, at eight years old, that it doesn't matter how grim the weather is in the UK, once the plane breaks through the dark, stormy clouds, you will always be met with a perfect blue sky because the clouds can only go so high and that's what blocks the sun.

This blew my mind and suddenly I wasn't so scared – I even got brave enough to press my face against the plastic window looking down at the clouds below.

The science behind the power of awe

According to research, experiencing true awe can make us more compassionate, less selfish, more curious, increase our connectedness with others and give us a sense of spiritual elevation. It can also increase positivity, reduce stress and decrease materialism.

The research by Keltner and Haidt which formed their 2003 paper 'Approaching awe, a moral, spiritual, and aesthetic emotion', showed that experiencing awe helps deactivate the default mode network, which is the part of your brain that remains active when you're not focused on the world around you. Keltner describes this network as the ego, and awe, he says, 'quiets that'.

Awe also stimulates the vagus nerve, which runs from the brain, through the face, down each side of the neck and on to the abdomen, and regulates our heart rates and digestive and respiratory systems. One of its many functions is as the main parasympathetic nerve in the body which sends a message to the body to calm down and relax. (This is one to remember if you're ever on a daytime quiz show . . . make sure you split your winnings with me.)

New adventures

Since the move to the countryside, there have been plenty of opportunities to experience awe. Studies show that going on a fifteen-minute 'awe walk' each day where we truly stop and appreciate nature and the world around us can boost positive emotions and ease stress.

I have been putting the wellies on and exploring the local area, sometimes with company, other times on my own. There's something that excites me every time I see a sign saying 'public footpath' as I enjoy the unknown of where it will take me and what I might discover, so I like to test them all out and see where I end up.

I purposely set no time that I need to be back for, I just get lost. And in doing so I've come across so many great spots of natural beauty like hidden lakes, old follies (broken old overgrown buildings), old Roman roads and even a huge hill surrounded by woodland which, when I'm feeling fit and up for it, I venture up to take in the incredible panoramic views in all directions.

I've been up there for sunrises, sunsets, summer picnics and winter hikes, and every single time it brings me that sense of gratitude for my surroundings.

Practising gratitude, the art of giving thanks, has become an important part of my life and pretty crucial to my overall sense of wellbeing. Psychological studies show that it is associated with increased happiness, improved health, a better ability to deal with adversity and strengthening relationships. So it feels like a no-brainer to me!

Being able to take all of that in alone or sharing it with others is a great feeling, and although most of the visitors we've had to stay since moving here curse me for making them climb the hill, their grins at the end show me how glad they are that they made it to the top without trying to kill me before they reached the summit.

Gimme five . . . ways to practise gratitude in nature

1. Find a peaceful space and set an intention for the day. Say it out loud (no one's listening, I promise!).

2. Give back by volunteering with a local conservation group to plant trees, litter-pick or tidy up green space.

3. Keep a daily gratitude diary and write it while in your favourite outdoor spot. List three things you're thankful for each day, however small.

4. Start a gratitude jar. Collect one item every time you take a walk in nature, whether that's a rock, a leaf, a shell or a pine cone, and keep them in a jar at home as a visual reminder of the everyday beauty outside.

5. Take time to stop and appreciate nature every day. Focus on one thing and notice how all your senses are responding to it.

How to build an awe walk into your daily routine

An awe walk is basically a mindful stroll in nature where you intentionally shift your focus from inward to outward, ground yourself in the present and soak up everything around you. It only needs to be fifteen minutes but it has to be focused and meaningful for you to really feel the benefit.

1. Decide on a location. It might be a local park or some woodland, anywhere you're going to be able to immerse yourself in the natural world.

2. Set a time each day to do this and don't let anything get in the way of it. Whatever you're in the middle of you can return to later. You might want to go first thing in the morning as the sun is coming up, or a moonlit walk underneath the stars might be more appealing.

3. Switch that mobile to Do Not Disturb mode or flight mode, or if you're really feeling it, turn it off completely.

4. Before you set off, some gentle breathing exercises will help make sure you are fully present. Box breathing is very simple to do – breathe in for four, hold for four, exhale for four and hold for four and repeat this four times.

5. Off you go, walking slowly to really drink in all of your surroundings. No need to rush! In fact, the whole point of an awe walk is not to rush at all.

My name is Joe and I'm an opacarophile

I really enjoy witnessing a sunrise as part of my new early morning routine, but to me, nothing beats a sunset. I'm an absolute sucker for a sunset.

This sounds like something corny you would write on a Tinder bio (along with the classic 'long walks on the beach' line) if you had nothing witty to put, but in my case it's true! And better than simply writing 'I'm an opacarophile' because that's probably going to get you no swipe rights.

But I am indeed an opacarophile and a proud one, too. The meaning of this word, by the way, is a person who loves sunsets. They never fail to inspire awe in me.

And they take me to a place mentally that is extremely calm, where I am at ease with myself, and it reassures me with thoughts like: 'Hey, see! There's no need to worry about sorting the tyres out on the car or making sure you've arranged your plans for Christmas or that deadline you've missed . . . Why worry when you have such a beautiful natural phenomenon in front of you? Just enjoy it and I'll return later to make you feel worried about deadlines, diseases and everything else before you go to sleep tonight.'

Thanks, mind, how very kind of you.

I think the reason I love sunsets so much is that I associate so many good memories around them and I've never seen two the same – they are forever changing based on the many conditions that make them what they are.

It always happens in the evening (obviously), so you can even treat yourself to a glass of wine whilst watching the sun go down.

Sorry to get morbid, but much like ourselves, they don't last for very long, not in the grand scheme of things anyway, so to be there and catch one in time feels quite special to me.

I always feel that once I've watched the sun pass then that usually gives me a sense of grounding, too. It makes me put a lot of stuff into perspective. This beautiful occurrence happens every day right across our planet and has done way before we got here and will continue to do so long after we're all gone.

Thinking about deep stuff like that can scare you a little, but it now gives me a good sense of gratitude for this ball of land and water we call Planet Earth.

Due to where my career has led me, I've been fortunate enough to witness a good ol' sunset in many different places around the globe. I even used to keep a folder on my old phone of all the best sunsets I'd seen, ranked in order from best to good (there is no such thing as a bad sunset in my eyes), with a photo for reference and any fun memories attached to that evening or time in general.

Six of the best: my all-time favourite sunsets

1. **The Maldives**

   The sort of place you'd expect the sunset of dreams, and it does not disappoint.

2. **Bunbury, Australia**

   The sunset on the beach near Dianne's parents' house is the best one we've seen as a couple. We had the whole beach to ourselves as it happened.

3. **Agnes Water and Town of 1770, Australia**

   When travelling with my friends we did something called 'scooteroo', which is essentially driving mini Harley Davidsons while looking for kangaroos. We stopped off at a harbour and watched a very dramatic sunset just as we saw a storm cloud coming in and raced back to avoid getting soaked . . . we got soaked.

4. **Lion's Head, South Africa**

   I climbed a mountain on New Year's Day to watch the sunset with friends and it was a memorable one. Climbing down before it got too dark was a bit of an adventure, too . . .

5. **Bowden Hill, Wiltshire**

   Watching the sunset over the village I grew up in will never not be special to me.

6. **Fiji**

   The best sunset I've ever witnessed. It set over a smaller island out at sea and the whole sky was pure red.

Some of the best sunsets I've witnessed were in my home county of Wiltshire as a child. Our parents' bedroom faced west and we were on a hill, so every once in a while, you'd hear Mum call out: 'Kids, come and look at this!' and we'd rush upstairs thinking: 'Uh-oh, the daffodil thief is back,' but luckily we were welcomed with the view of a sunset that made the sky look like it was on fire.

Living in the now

I'm a big believer in the saying 'different strokes for different folks', not just because it makes me feel like a wise old wizard when I manage to slip it into conversations, but also because it lends itself well to the use of social media and being in the moment.

I certainly have my preference and a way I like to do things and manage how best to make the most of being in said moment. I've never understood why people will happily stand outside in a field full of other humans on 5 November and spend the entire fireworks display filming the show rather than watching it for real. I've also never EVER heard of anyone watching back their fireworks video (or showing it to anyone else for that matter) or jumping for joy to watch a display through a phone screen. It's recorded and then never looked at again because a fireworks display is supposed to be enjoyed in the moment.

But hey, different strokes for different folks. However, the people who film an entire music concert tip me over the edge. I'm telling you, the Draft Savers movement is the way to go on this.

I may feel this way because I'm quite a nostalgic person, but I do feel quite passionately that life is one big trial and error, and in time, we'll be led down the path that's best for us.

I've missed out on trying new things and haven't made the most of what's right in front of me due to social media, despite the fact it's a brilliant tool for discovering new things in the first place. Take a step back now and again, be self-aware and find the balance of what works best for you. But stop filming fireworks.

Gimme five . . . ways to be more present in nature

1. Stop to touch the nature around you – the tree trunks, the sand, the crunchy leaves, the water, the rocks. Notice their texture, their temperature and how they make you feel.

2. Listen for the birdsong, the swishing of the trees, the trickling of a stream, the blowing of the breeze.

3. Go out on your own so you can really try to find peace, quieten the mind and focus.

4. Breathe deeply and mindfully. Take in the smells of the plants, the weather, the earth. Or that weird but lovely smell of well-overdue rain on hot roads or pathways.

5. Try walking barefoot. This is obviously more appealing on a warm beach, but doing it in a forest or on grass or any other natural surface allows you to feel different sensations and can help you feel more connected to the earth.

Trying new things

Getting out of your comfort zone is always going to feel unnerving at first. I've spent my whole life finding it difficult to start something new, whether that's secondary school, joining the rugby team, a new direction with my online content or even this book. It took me nearly an hour to write the very first sentence. Great – I'd managed to get the dreaded writer's block before I'd even typed a solitary word.

But just because I've always found it hard to start something new, doesn't mean that it's not extremely enjoyable and rewarding once I get going. Without getting all 'self-help-y' and 'inspirational quote-y' on you, nothing worth having comes easy. If you cruise through life on easy mode are you really living?

And doing things that scare you a little is actually really good for you and could give you that much-needed dose of awe . . . as long as it's legal and not something that puts your life in danger, of course!

In 2011, I decided I wanted to take a short three-month break from my thatching apprenticeship to go and see as much of the other side of the world as possible, backpacking with two of my best mates from school.

I can remember taking the afternoon off from working in the barn preparing materials for the roof and walking into STA Travel (leaving a trail of bits of straw all over their carpet) and taking the plunge and booking a gap-year backpackers' trip to Thailand, Singapore, Australia, New Zealand, Fiji and finally a quick stop at LA before heading back home.

I still lived at home with my parents and sister, I had a job I loved and a good solid routine, so it was time to scare myself a little and have a bit of a challenge doing something that felt very alien. There's a part in our minds where we can get too comfortable with having things done for us, and that was exactly where I was at.

I have hundreds of stories I could tell you from those months of travelling, from eating scorpions on the side of the road in Bangkok to nearly being eaten alive by dingos in Australia. That trip is a book in itself.

I came back a completely different person but in the best way possible. I had seen things beyond my imagination, met other travellers who we would swap stories with and seen how other cultures lived. I also skydived and bungee jumped in New Zealand and took a surfboard out into shark-infested waters in Australia and ventured to a night market in Bangkok.

None of those things was easy for me, because I'm not a natural risk-taker, but I'm so glad I got to try these new experiences which, along with the trip itself, shaped me into a more independent, appreciative, contented person.

I've kept that going right the way through, and finding new things to try has become a constant theme in my life and career.

For example, I had never taken yoga seriously before meeting Dianne. She's a dedicated 'yogi' and asked if I wanted to come along with her to a 'hot yoga flow' class down the road from where we were living at the time in Clapham.

I agreed and thought I'd give it my best shot but unfortunately for me, it wasn't what I was expecting. At all.

I think it was the point where the instructor asked people to raise their hand if they were new to hot yoga flow and I was the only one in the thirty-strong class to raise my hand, that I realized I'd bitten off a little more than I could chew.

I'm still not sure how I managed to survive that class. For all I know I may well have passed out five minutes in, but not only did I feel incredible walking out into the cold air afterwards, but it was the beginning of a really fun hobby that I now enjoy with Dianne regularly – we practise together in the garden during the warmer months and I love that.

Over time I've actually gotten better at it and I can really see the benefits both physically and mentally. It gives me grounding and calm and has become a great way for me to de-stress and practise mindfulness and gratitude.

Along with the new-found love of paddle boarding (and, of course, dancing) it shows we can always find new activities to take pleasure in. While I'm definitely no duck to water in any of them to begin with, the feelings of enjoyment and mastery which come from the development of learning a new skill do wonders for my wellbeing.

So next time you see an advert for pole vaulting lessons in your local newsagent window, have a second thought about it before you dismiss it.

The best advice I can really give you is to do everything at your own pace. It's not a race to see who can take on the most hobbies and prove to everyone else that they're doing the most cool unique things online.

But every now and then, take the right turn when you usually go left. Or next time you see a public footpath sign that you've always walked past, try going down it for once and see where it takes you. Hopefully somewhere awe-some (sorry, couldn't resist).

Seriously though, finding awe – the most positive and powerful of all the emotions – in the everyday, can stimulate, heal and inspire. And by immersing ourselves in nature, we have a much greater chance of experiencing the full force of it and everything it has to offer.

Go get it!

Chapter 7

HUMAN NATURE

There is a moment that stands out to me as the point when I had a bit of a breakthrough in learning the importance of real-life connections and relationships.

I've always said that Dianne was my first ever girlfriend, a statement I still stand by. But technically – and sorry Dianne if you're reading this – I had a girlfriend for a whole weekend when I was thirteen.

There, I said it. I'm sorry I lied. Now, you'd think there's nothing wrong with having a girlfriend at thirteen. Young love and so on. BUT, bizarrely, I had never met this girl in person before we went 'official'. Our relationship was purely developed and established through MSN and text messages.

I remember that I had 'met' this girl through a mutual friend, who I actually did know in real life and so could vouch that she was indeed a real person . . . phew.

Unfortunately, I'm not too certain on how the conversations went or how we got to the point of deciding we were now officially 'going out' with each other, even though to actually 'go out' with someone you surely need to see them in person to actually, um, 'go out'. Even more comically, I think she lived in a completely different part of the UK. So you could say it was doomed from the start. And you would be right.

Peer pressure from my mates, who also had online girlfriends they'd never met (I'm starting to think it must have been the cool thing to do back then), and the safety barrier of being behind a keyboard and screen, gave me a sense of confidence. Or that feeling we now know in the twenty-first century as YOLO.

I took the plunge and accepted the offer to be her boyfriend. Yes, that's right, she asked me. I said I had confidence while behind the comfort of a screen and keyboard, but not that much confidence, OK?

We were official for a grand total of the weekend. Pathetic, I know, but it did lead me to have a life-defining moment of realization and clarity. I had just got a girlfriend, for the first time, and I felt . . . nothing. It didn't feel special in any way. I actually started to feel a bit panicky, if I'm honest.

This meant if things carried on, I was going to have to meet up with her in person and what if she'd lied about her hobbies and interests or worse – her height! I'd spent a lot of time talking to this girl, but what if it was different in real life?

I remember that whole weekend feeling all over the place in my head and not really being able to put a finger on why.

Meanwhile, back in the real world . . .

That Sunday, my dad took me to the local river to go fishing. In hindsight, our trip came at the perfect time.

'This will take my mind off the uneasy feeling,' I thought just as a text came through from the girl because I hadn't replied to her last one within five minutes. I decided to leave my Nokia (I used to call it a Rokia because it was tough enough to double up as an actual rock) in the car for once and lugged the fishing gear towards the riverbank with my dad in the hope that it would solve everything.

This fishing trip with my dad was extremely special to me. Even more special than our first fishing trip together when we managed to catch nothing all day until we were packing the van up and I managed to reel in the biggest goldfish you've ever seen.

To this day I'm still convinced it was someone's unwanted pet they tried to offload into the nearest lake where it decided it was going to have its own montage moment and get so big that it grew legs and was able to march its way on land all the way back to the lousy owner's house and give them what for.

Anyway, as I was saying, this fishing trip was better than that. Why so? Because it was the first time in ages that I had chosen for myself to take a break from the screens and the online stuff and just enjoy what was around me. Real-life things.

The walk along the riverbank arguing with my dad over where the best spot was. Casting my bait straight into weeds. Sitting patiently waiting for a bite. Dipping in and out of conversation with my dad, sometimes just sitting in silence taking in nature and appreciating it. And it was so refreshing and cleansing for me.

Looking back now, it was a powerful fusion of the need for nature (our biophilia) with the need for human connection. Proper human connection.

And combining the two things we are hardwired to yearn for can be the very definition of life-affirming.

It was certainly exactly what I needed in that moment. It cemented the father–son bond, which does make it sound quite clichéd, but it's true.

Studies by the University of Illinois have shown that combining nature with loved ones can significantly strengthen family bonds.

Researchers Dina Izenstark and Aaron Ebata took mother and daughter pairs who were told to go for a walk either outside or around a shopping mall.

They discovered that of the two, it was the walk in nature which clearly increased positive interactions among the pairs.

It was also found that the nature setting was where the mothers and daughters showed greater cohesion, closeness, a sense of unity, and the ability to get along.

How amazing is that?

Making connections in nature

I remember when we were lucky enough to have a couple of snow days from school. As a lot of you will know, the UK doesn't respond to extreme weather very well (we're great at talking/moaning about it, though) and everything tends to grind to a halt with the lightest dusting of snow.

I was ecstatic that I didn't have to prepare for my mock exams in school and instead I could pretend to do it at home and go sledging and mess about in the snow.

I noticed that being out and about in nature at this time, whoever you bumped into, you instantly had a conversation starter and everyone seemed to share the same excitement. I ended up ganging up with all the locals in my tiny village (people who on a regular day without the eight inches of snow, I definitely wouldn't be hanging out with) and getting to know loads of people I wouldn't normally speak to.

And although we were still getting our phones out here and there to film each other trying to stand up on our sledges going down a hill dangerously fast, it was too cold to have the mobiles out for long and we were all just enjoying the moment together.

Back to the fishing trip. We also caught one of the biggest barbel in Wiltshire that evening which I'm putting down to the fact that it was nature's way of rewarding me for appreciating it and absorbing it all.

After this awakening of sorts, I decided to call it off with MSN messenger girl who I won't name in this book. If you are reading this, then I hope you are well and I'm sorry I didn't text you back sooner, but I was busy being a biophile, soz xox.

My top tips for using nature to nourish your relationships

1. Go for a walk and choose a location with limited reception so the temptation to check in on various platforms is removed. Remember, you're a Draft Saver now.

2. Start a nature project together. It could be something in the garden (never a bad thing to get an extra pair of hands with the weeding, all in the name of 'bonding'), a birdwatching expedition or a crafting session using materials gathered from the outdoors.

3. If there's something you've wanted to try for a while (wild swimming, kayaking or barefoot running) but have been putting off, see if you can rope a friend into joining you. Sharing new experiences with someone you care about can make them even more fulfilling.

4. Book a proper back to basics camping adventure with a big group of your nearest and dearest.

5. Sign up to a charity challenge with a friend or relative, perhaps something you have to train for together. Visit www.charitychallenge.com to find something which will work for you.

6. Take a picnic somewhere with a beautiful backdrop – a waterfall, a lakeside or on the beach if you don't mind the odd bit of sand in your sandwich. The National Trust has a list of the best picnic spots in the UK (www.nationaltrust.org.uk).

7. Find out if there are any community gardening projects in your local area and volunteer with a loved one. The Royal Horticultural Society will be able to point you in the right direction (www.rhs.org.uk).

Back to the balancing act

I really wanted to bring everything I've talked about in this book back to this point and to reinforce the importance of finding a balance between the online socializing (which can be great) and the real-life connections which are so vital, whether they're with humans or with nature or – even better – with both at the same time.

Growing up in the MSN era was exciting and, as I touched on previously, I did spend a lot of my time sitting on an uncomfortable old wooden chair waiting for my friends to come online so I could ask them the same questions day in day out like 'wuu2?' (what are you up to?) and 'wubu2?' (what you been up to?).

Deep stuff, right? I think there was an acronym for that, too – 'DMC', which stood for deep and meaningful conversation. It was as if we were talking in code like robots.

(I did inadvertently end up teaching myself how to touch-type, though. It's a skill I still use to this day and it has definitely made this book easier to write and less daunting. So not a complete waste of time!)

I made these new 'friendships', such as the one with the aforementioned girlfriend, but I put that word in inverted commas because it's now very apparent that although they may have felt it at the time, they were not real relationships. Not the sorts of relationships that humans have been used to and developed over millennia.

Teeing up a new hobby

Studies have shown that people who are more socially connected to their family, friends or community are generally happier, physically healthier and live longer with fewer mental health problems compared to people who are less socially connected to the people around them.

I totally get this. I spend a lot of my time checking the WhatsApp group chat to keep up with my close friends in Wiltshire, and I love all the various funny memes being posted or watching a debate unfold over something ridiculous.

But no matter what is shared in that group chat, nothing beats actually meeting up with them and socializing face to face. And on reflection, I would say that 80 per cent of the chat in these groups is reminiscing and chatting about funny moments when we've been together or planning the next meet-up.

We're all at that age where we have either taken up golf or have had major FOMO and bought a set of clubs and come along to play (I use the term 'play' very loosely for some of them), but for all of us we love getting together and enjoying a round together.

To be honest, the actual golf becomes a bit of a by-product to me. I'm not much good at it, but I will never refuse a round because for us it's a chance to catch up, take the piss out of each other, get a bit of exercise in and just enjoy our surroundings for eighteen holes.

Golf courses are designed to be walked around and it's like having a whole park to yourself. I've always found it a very peaceful place, and when playing with my mates the only time the phone comes out the golf bag is to capture a tee off by the one in our group who you know is going to make a hash of it.

We always completely lose track of time when we get together on a golf course which I see as a good thing. We all benefit from spending time together as a bunch of mates outdoors in beautiful surroundings and with the occasional inquisitive goose.

The key to living a longer and happier life?

I remember once watching a television show about a town in Italy called Acciaroli where they had the highest number of centenarians in a population of around 2,000 people. An amazing one in ten people were 100 or older which was 500 times the number in the UK.

What stood out to me most about this programme, other than the people all being very old, was that there was such a sense of community. Every door was left unlocked and they all would visit each other and spend all day in the company of friends, family and neighbours.

Some of the residents there claimed that the key to a long life was living by the coast and the sea air keeping them feeling young or the Mediterranean diet consisting of a lot of fresh fish, vegetables and olive oil. All good points. But another clear factor lay in their social behaviours with the high levels of human interaction.

It's been really fun since moving to the countryside to host my friends from all over – I get so excited to take them for walks and through the woods and the fields.

Initially I thought they might just find it boring and muddy. But every time I've taken mates out for a stroll in the countryside we now call home, they have absolutely loved it. It's such a good opportunity to chat to each other and reconnect.

It may sound a bit odd, but I've also noticed that silences aren't awkward at all when going for a stroll in nature. I can definitely be a bit socially awkward at times but I've yet to feel that way whilst going for a walk with mates and the conversation goes quiet. Enjoying a walk together can be just as powerful and meaningful as having an intense, deep conversation.

Taking time out to experience more things like this, whether that's going for a stroll in the park with a friend, a bracing walk battling the elements on a windy British beach or spending forty-five minutes trembling trying to stand up on a paddle board without plunging into icy cold water with no Brighton sharks in, is never a waste of time. They can all leave you feeling stronger and more alive.

I'm going to make a wild comparison here, so stay with me (this may not work), but as humans we're all a bit like those fragile houseplants we try so desperately to keep watered correctly, get the soil just right for and give the right amount of sunlight to.

I'm sure these houseplants, in their correct climates, are designed and evolved to thrive in their natural habitat, but if you're anything like one of my many rubber plants, you won't cope so well with being inside and stuck in a pot on your own all the time.

What I'm trying to say (I guess) is that we are sensitive beings, and sometimes logging off and being out in nature with friends and the people we love is the best remedy to make us feel our good old selves again.

Set aside some time to nurture and invest in yourself and your relationships, just like you would with your favourite houseplant.

Sometimes it can be quite tricky to put into words how certain things make you feel, but although we are advancing rather quickly into the future with communication and technology and it looks like we could all be playing virtual strip table tennis with Mark Zuckerberg in the metaverse in a few years' time, there is still a magical sweet spot.

Get the balance right between screen time and scene time (see what I did there? Can we print that on a shirt or what?), re-establish a connection with the natural world around you, give your over-worked squidgy pink brains a rest (I presume it's pink, I've never seen a brain that's not a cartoon one, sorry), know when to switch off, practise gratitude, meditation or whatever floats your boat and you will be on to a winner. Not just in your relationships with the people around you, but also with yourself.

Get outside, soak it up, fill your lungs and fill your boots! Feel appreciation for the magnificence of nature and take full advantage of its restorative powers. Embrace it all and more importantly, enjoy it.

There really is no time like the present.

So, there we go. We've made it! I feel like we've covered an awful lot of ground together and I genuinely hope that you can take something away from this.

I certainly have, just from writing it. This book has been in my head for a while now and it's felt empowering and hugely satisfying finally getting it all down.

Even though (ironically enough) I have written this entire book while looking at my laptop screen, it's been very therapeutic and has felt productive for me. Knowing that I've created something that you guys might use to make life feel a little easier is pretty incredible. And the thought that you have taken the time to read it really is the cherry on top of this cake of pleasantness which the experience has been for me.

I have unlocked lots of fond memories from growing up and recalled and reflected on valuable information that I've picked up over the years. From reconnecting with nature to finding out what exactly awe actually means and why we feel it, and why, from time to time, we bloody hecking well need it, hopefully there's some good stuff in there that you can take for yourselves and even pass on to others.

Having built my career around social media it would be silly for me to bash it and tell you that if you keep scrolling you're going down a one-way road to living your worst life.

Let's be honest, I wouldn't be writing this book if it wasn't for spending an awful lot of my time online building a social following. So I don't want you to think that you need to bury your mobile in the garden and revert back to the landline times.

It's about learning to embrace the new digital world we live in, but also reminding ourselves how important it is to switch off from it and take some time out to ground ourselves back in nature.

That's what helps us put things into perspective and makes us feel great physically and mentally – always has done and always will, regardless of the latest amazing tech discovery that's going to transform our lives.

Striking the balance that works best for you is key. We're all different, and we're all going to have different balance points. So, while I've shared some of the things that worked for me, I'd urge you to keep going and explore the things that will work for you. Find your own happy medium and have fun doing it!

Thank you so much for reading this book. I really hope you keep coming back to it to refresh what we have learnt together.

And let me know how you're getting on! Share your awe walks, your discoveries, your gardens, your sunsets, your attempts at paddle boarding and – please! – any genius tips for keeping those flipping rubber plants alive.

This is a busy, buzzy, high-pressured world. We're all trying to find our feet and catch our breath and no one has all the answers.

But if you want to escape the noise, let go of stress and restore some peace, calm and balance into your life, then taking everything back to nature is the perfect place to start.

Thank You

It has been such a fun and enjoyable process creating this book. It would not have been possible without the incredible team at Penguin. Fenella Bates you have been a star from the very first Zoom meeting, giving me the confidence to throw myself into this project and make it the best it could be. Dan Prescott-Bennett and Sarah Fraser you have made this book look beautiful and a must-have for coffee tables everywhere. The editing and production team, Agatha Russell, Beatrix McIntyre, Xanthea Johnson, Sarah Bance, Fiona Brown and Alice Mottram, thank you for keeping me on track. Thanks to Beth Neil, I feel like I may still be on chapter one if it wasn't for your guidance through our weekly Zooms. Also, thank you to Ella Watkins and Steph Biddle for sharing what we've created with as many people as possible. Thanks to Dan Kennedy for the incredible photographs. Thanks to Emma Leon, Annie Swain, Emma LaHaye and Lauren Kay for making me look cool and handsome.

Thanks to my team at WME, Matilda Forbes Watson and Matthew Harvey. My friends and family and beautiful girlfriend Dianne Buswell, who inspire me daily and are always so supportive of my creativity. Lastly, thank you to you for purchasing this book. I really hope it becomes one you return to again and again for help to find balance, restore your connectivity with nature and ultimately look after yourself.

Picture Credits

The author and publisher would like to thank all copyright holders for permission to reproduce their work. Every effort has been made to trace copyright holders and to obtain their permission for the use of copyright material. The publisher apologises for any errors or omissions and would be grateful to be notified of any corrections that should be incorporated in future editions of this book.

Internal photography and front cover © Dan Kennedy

91 © Brett Jordan/Unsplash

114–5, 118, 126–7, 152, 231 © Shutterstock

124–5 © Rebrandy

All other images and illustrations courtesy of the author

The author would like to thank Niwaki (niwaki.com) and Labour & Wait (www. labourandwait.co.uk) for the loan of tools and items for this book.

michael joseph

UK | USA | Canada | Ireland | Australia
India | New Zealand | South Africa

Michael Joseph is part of the Penguin
Random House group of companies
whose addresses can be found at
global.penguinrandomhouse.com.

Penguin
Random House
UK

First published in Great Britain
by Michael Joseph, 2022

001

Set in Futura LT Pro, Orpheus Pro and Calder

Colour reproduction by Altaimage Ltd
Printed in Italy by Printer Trento Ltd S.r.L.

A CIP catalogue record for this book is
available from the British Library

ISBN: 978–0–241–56576–6

www.greenpenguin.co.uk

MIX
Paper from
responsible sources
FSC
www.fsc.org
FSC® C018179

Penguin Random House is committed to a
sustainable future for our business, our readers
and our planet. This book is made from Forest
Stewardship Council® certified paper.